A SCIENTIST'S QUEST FOR GOD IN DAILY LIFE

Dr Darrel Ho-Yen

BMSc(Hons) MBChB FRCPath

MD DSc

DODONA BOOKS

Copyright © Darrel O Ho-Yen, 2003

ISBN 0-9511090-6-5

Published and distributed by:

Dodona Books
Corriemuir
Viewhill
Culloden Moor
Inverness
IV2 5EA
(www.dodonabooks.co.uk)

**British Library Cataloging in
Publication Data**
A catalogue record of this book is
available from the British Library.

Printed in Great Britain by Highland Printers, Inverness

CONTENTS

ABOUT THE AUTHOR

Dr Darrel Ho-Yen, BMSc(Hons) MBChB FRCPath MD DSc was born in Guyana, South America, but finished his schooling in London. After Voluntary Services Overseas in the Caribbean, he studied at Dundee University medical school. He completed his training at the Regional Virus Laboratory, Ruchill Hospital, Glasgow. He is now Head of Microbiology at Raigmore Hospital, Inverness, Director of the Scottish Toxoplasma Reference Laboratory, and Honorary Clinical Senior Lecturer at Aberdeen University.

Dr Ho-Yen has had extensive experience in managing and counselling patients with Post Viral Fatigue Syndrome and the first edition of "Better Recovery from Viral Illnesses" (1985) was the first book on the subject. (2nd edition 1987; 3rd edition 1993, reprinted 1994; 4th edition 1999). He has written many other books: co-author of "Diseases of Infection" (1987,1993) and co-editor of "Human Toxoplasmosis" (1992), both published by Oxford University Press; co-author of "Ticks", Mercat Press (1998); and section editor of "Science of Laboratory Diagnosis", ISIS Medical (1998).

His experience of the needs of patients with chronic illnesses prompted him to write "Unwind! Understand and control life, be better!!" (this book combines relaxation and stress management techniques) in 1991 (reprinted in 1994); and "Climbing Out of the Pit of Life" (this book deals with recovering from great loss) in 1995. Dr Ho-Yen has published numerous scientific papers and articles for medical practitioners and the general public, and lectures extensively.

PREFACE

Religious beliefs can be an important factor in the response to disease, and some patients lose their faith whilst others have it strengthened. I have often wondered what makes the difference. In my book, "Climbing Out of the Pit of Life", my thesis was that a person's response to bereavement was similar to that of any great loss such as disease, unemployment, divorce or failing an important exam. Such situations are a test of an individual's coping strategies. Equally, they are a test of one's religious beliefs.

This book records a test of my faith. It is a reflection of my own experiences and so quite different from my previous books. It has also been difficult to remain objective, but in some ways a book like this must be subjective. Nevertheless, I tried to apply the same approach and discipline as in my other books.

I have been very fortunate in having great support as I have written this book. My sons, Gregory and Colan, have been very tolerant and understanding. As always, my good friend, Alan Bowley, has been his usual pernickety and out-spoken self, but again his comments have often been annoyingly correct. I am very grateful to the Reverend Doctor Iain Macritchie for being very generous in his criticisms, and for long, animated discussions over coffee and lunch. My longsuffering colleagues, Dr Jean Chatterton, Dr David Ashburn, Dr

7

Roger Evans and Ms Marilyn Davidson have been excellent at proof reading and commenting on the manuscript. In addition, Dr David Ashburn has undertaken the daunting task of coordinating my efforts with the printers with tremendous optimism and efficiency. As in the past, Mr Forbes Cunningham of Highland Printers has been exceedingly good-humoured and helpful; he is what all printers should be! Lastly and most importantly, Mrs Barbara Reed has been very brave in volunteering to prepare this manuscript through its many drafts; she has been unflappable, resilient and extremely efficient.

Dr Darrel Ho-Yen
February 2003

CHAPTER ONE

INTRODUCTION

On 1st October 1994, I returned from an international conference in Germany to find that my wife had moved out of our home. My two sons greeted me with anguish on their faces, and I felt hopelessly out of my depth. I wanted to feel sorry for myself and wallow in self-pity. However, a household needs to be run and there are always jobs to be done. I made the decision that my sons and I would do all that was necessary to sustain ourselves. The house jobs were divided up and over the weeks a good routine developed.

My wife had left because she had become involved in a local church and wanted to be closer to God. I was interfering with the way that she wanted to worship, and she wanted her freedom. She felt that it was all very simple and straightforward; I should accept her decision and get on with my own life.

1. Early life

I was born in British Guiana (now Guyana) and went to primary school later than my classmates. The school was Saint Gabriel's School run by the Convent of the Good Shepherd. The Church of England nuns were very strict. Each day we spent time in the chapel attached to the school. It is said that if the Jesuits teach a youngster for seven years, then that person would believe in their

God for life. The nuns taught me for four years, and I doubt that I can ever be free from their influence.

When I was 11 years old, my brother and I attended confirmation classes at the Saint James-the-Less Church at Kitty, East Coast Demerara, British Guiana. The priest, Joseph H Jones, was a strict man who insisted that we attend church regularly and we took our studies seriously. On Sundays, I can still remember the feeling of being woken from a deep sleep at 5.15 am to get dressed and attend a 6.00 am service. In November 1960, we were confirmed into the Church of England and I felt that I had strong Christian beliefs.

In 1962, when there were widespread riots and British troops were called to maintain order, my father felt that the family's lives were threatened. We emigrated to London. It is a hard thing to sell up all of one's possessions and move to a different country. My father had received his higher education in Canada and wanted to emigrate there. However, he was influenced by our schooling being similar to the English model and so we moved to London.

Even in spring, I found London cold. We were the only Chinese in the neighbourhood and racism was open and widespread. The people were not friendly and the smog had a queer smell. The local church reflected the weather and was unwelcoming. My father found employment difficult. Despite having a BSc(Hons) and MSc from McGill University, he could not find a job. Many times he was told he was 'overqualified' for jobs. He was unemployed for six months before he finally found a job as a teacher in a Secondary Modern School. These were hard times. I ceased to believe in the established Church.

Our savings were greatly depleted by my father's unemployment, but he refused to claim unemployment (dole) money. When he got a job, we started to look for a house to buy. Although we had the deposit and could get a mortgage, many people refused to sell us their houses. We were even told that: "this was not a neighbourhood for Chinese families". This deeply wounded my mother and it was only many years later that I realised how difficult she found our existence. In British Guiana, we had a big house, servants, a position in society, good friends and all the family. In London, we shared two rooms and my mother cooked in her bedroom.

My life was schoolwork and sport. Although I did well in my mock 'O' levels, I got terrible results in the real examinations. I was learning that this was not a fair world. The cycle was repeated in my 'A' levels, and I became convinced that you had to depend on only yourself. My only good memories were of long hot days playing cricket or cool summer evenings on the tennis court. Joy was in the physical activity and in the enjoyment of my skills.

2. Later life

Eventually I got some good 'A' levels, but I had to have a gap year as the University system only considered my previous exam results. I was sent to Jamaica to teach on Voluntary Service Overseas. Although I did lots of extra teaching in illiteracy classes and at the Polio Rehabilitation Centre, I found the work very easy. Then, there were the parties: 6-7 on a Saturday night was quite usual. Sundays were for the beach with swimming, sleeping and eating. The sunsets were wonderful and one never tired of watching the end-of-day performance. However, the most memorable moments were the weekend hikes, especially into the Blue Mountains which were famed for their coffee. Here the climate was temperate, but still the sweat poured off with the climb. We would stop and have a grapefruit freshly cut from the tree; and we would spend the night sleeping on a wooden pew in the local church.

University life was like a jungle full of challenges and pitfalls. I loved it. The diversity of people, the heated arguments and the unanswerable questions were everywhere. Political debates and the solutions to world problems were far more interesting than academic work. In contrast, the religious groups such as the Christian Union and the Catholic Society appeared afraid. They refused to go into the jungle and instead stayed at the periphery where it was safe. I perceived this unwillingness to embrace life to the full as a weakness: lack of faith in God and in themselves.

The year after graduation, I got married. The stimulation of University life was replaced by work, children and studying for exams. There was never enough time; always jobs to be done and people to see. Work was not straightforward and we had to move from Dundee to Glasgow and then to Inverness. Finally, in 1987 I was appointed Consultant Microbiologist and Director of the

Scottish Toxoplasma Reference Laboratory at Raigmore Hospital, Inverness. My job was to provide medical clinical services and undertake scientific research. Over the years, the Department produced very many publications with several books and numerous scientific papers. Good science was being done.

Time for work, children and social commitments always seemed greater than that available. Then, my wife started several cycles of church for a few years followed by hill-walking for a few years. My sons and I were infrequent participants of both. My Christian beliefs were weak and hill walking had become a chore. There was little time for reflection. But life was productive and progress seemed to be made by all family members. The holidays were fantastic and were a just reward for hard work by all. Life was very good. All had appeared to be well.

Conclusion

In 1994, as I approached fifty years of age, my life was thrown into chaos. I was forced to examine my religious beliefs. The firm Christian beliefs of my youth had been modified to cope with living in the "real world". I had reached a position where religion was peripheral and was "fitted in" to my busy life. I was not living my beliefs. I knew that I was like lots of other people, but was this right? I had believed that my life was "good" but now I had to reassess what this meant. I hoped that my 24 years of scientific research would help me to ask the right questions, and I would be able to take a systematic approach to finding answers.

CHAPTER TWO

THE WHOLE BIBLE

Was I the victim of God's injustice? Did God act like this? These questions plagued my mind. I did not know the answer. I reasoned that the problem was my knowledge. An objective assessment of my religious education would conclude that I had not left primary school. So, I resolved to do what I had always toyed with doing but which I could never find the time to undertake. I decided to read the whole Bible.

Resolve is one thing, but action is another. I kept thinking of how to do it. One friend suggested that I take a course, but I did not like courses. Another suggested that there were reading programmes which considered various biblical themes, but I felt that this meant skipping around the Bible. I finally decided that there was a certain attractive simplicity in reading this great book "cover to cover". So, on a cold dark night, on 1st February 1995, I started reading my New International Version of the Bible.

I started my journey through the Bible with great apprehension. Like starting medical school, I was scared but hoped if I stuck to it, I would get knowledge. A friend had said that he read the Bible in a year and it had meant you had to read 3 chapters a night. This sounded a large commitment and I realised why the great majority of Christians have never read the whole Bible. I seriously

14

wondered if this was one of those jobs that I would start but never finish.

1. Some answers.

I tried to be a good scientist. I made notes; I revised; and I linked my past work with my present. It became a pig's breakfast. As the weeks and months went by, the only certainty was that this was too big a job for a normal person. I kept thinking: "Why do you have to read the whole Bible?". The answer was so you did not miss anything - but was the effort worth the reward? I told myself that as I did not trust the Church or minister, I had to read all the data for myself. It was good science to see all the data. For a while, I was content. Then, I thought that I was reading a translation so someone had already tampered with the data. Late at night, this was too much, so I ignored this last thought.

My readings were not ideal. On Mondays, I took my time; by Fridays, I rushed my reading. In between, I was trying to cope with work, the household and my sons. At times, I got bored and spent more time contemplating how much I had to do. By the spring, I felt one thing: this was not the way one was supposed to read the Bible. My perception of reading the Bible as a peaceful, enlightening process was destroyed. It had become work... hard work. I prayed. Was it worth carrying on reading the way I had been? Would it be better to read single verses and contemplate their significance? What would God want? The answers surprised me.

The answers were not revelations. They did not come as

lightning bolts. But rather, they simply became more obvious as time (several weeks) went on:

a) There was no wrong way to read the Bible.

b) God wanted you to read the Bible; he did not mind if you were bored.

c) God was equally happy with you studying one verse as reading several chapters.

d) God wanted time and commitment, and what you achieved was secondary.

2. Covenants

The translation of the Hebrew into "covenant" can have several subtle meanings: promise, obligation, agreement, contract, pact or treaty. I readily identified with covenants as it was how I had reached agreements with my sons. "I now establish my covenant with you and your descendants after you" (Genesis 9.9) had a certainty that appealed to me. It seemed the way that things should be done.

I realised that my beliefs had not emphasised the importance of covenants. And so it was a major insight that God felt that this was a way of reaching an understanding with His people. I recognised that I had been more influenced by the teaching of God's love and His grace; I had to only receive. With covenants, I had to also agree to do. This seemed to me to be far more natural, and I liked having to have personal commitment.

16

It is estimated that there are 286 covenants in the Old Testament so it seemed a tried and tested way in which God did business. I recognised that there was a great diversity of covenants:

a)   between God and individuals: these might be imposed by God on himself (Genesis, 9.9) or on individuals (Hosea, 2.18).

b)   between God and nations: the covenant between God and the Israelites is special (Deuteronomy 29.1), but there may be demands on the Israelites (Genesis 17.1-14). Circumcision is not only one of these demands but is also an important sign (Genesis 17.11).

c)   between human parties: these are an extension of the agreements with God (Genesis 21.22-24). When the agreement is between nations, the term covenant is implied rather than used.

There is a sense that the covenants are binding obligations. Although there is a feeling of legality, the agreements are "ignored" (Proverbs 2.17) and "broken" (Hosea 6.7). I wondered if this was why God had given up making covenants in the New Testament – it simply did not work. Maybe God had decided that the best approach was not to have anything said or written down. He had tried these methods and they did not work. Instead He would simply let love and grace work through His people.

This greatly saddened me. I wanted covenants. It made

sense. Also, it meant that God would have to appear to me and negotiate the deal. As I always felt able to get a good deal, it also meant that I would have practical experience of how my God uses His brain. It seemed that this active exchange must be far superior to the passive approach of letting it all happen. Everyone knew that letting love take its course was a very unreliable way of doing anything.

Jeremiah mentions the "new" covenant: "The time is coming" declares the Lord "When I will make a new covenant" (31.31) which is "everlasting" (32.40). In the New Testament the new covenant is associated with the death of Christ, the Lord's Supper and the Eucharist: "This cup is the new covenant in my blood" (Luke 22.20). This new covenant also moves away from the law ("letter") to the "Spirit": "He has made us competent as ministers of a new covenant – not of the letter but of the Spirit" (2 Corinthinians 3.6).

It seemed to me that the new covenant was too all encompassing – it was like allowing someone (the people) to make direct debits to God. The direct debits were automatic and frequently forgotten. It would have been so much better if God made people pay in hard cash. This would make them appreciate the real position.

3.   Punishment

My father and the nuns brought me up in a climate of "Do not withhold discipline from a child.... punish him with the rod and save his soul from death". (Proverbs 23.13-14). I

18

accepted this and still believe this to be right. The relationship between God and myself is best described as that of a father and son. As my earthly father punished me, I also punished my sons. The role of punishment in the Old Testament made a great impression on me: "I will punish them for their sin" (Exodus 32.34); and "I will punish the world for its evil, the wicked for their sins" (Isaiah, 13.11). I also liked that there was a balance to the punishment: "I will punish you as your deeds deserve" (Jeremiah 21.14).

I loved the concept of an all-powerful God of justice and punishment of the Old Testament. As I approached the New Testament, I expected this position to be diluted with an emphasis on forgiveness and love. I learned that this expectation was simply how the New Testament had been quoted to me. The reality was that there was the same God in the New Testament: "It is mine to avenge; I will repay" (Romans 12.19); "He is God's servant, an agent to bring punishment on the wrongdoer" (Romans 13.4); and "to hold the unrighteous for the days of judgement while continuing their punishment" (2 Peter 2.9).

My reading of the Bible had allowed me to examine the data. In the past, selected quotations and interpretations had been fed to me. When I examined the data for myself, I appreciated more. God, the Father recognised the importance of punishment. This punishment was a result of knowledge and love, and in the hope that the recipient would learn. It was as a father would bring up a child.

4.   Ecclesiastes

After the demands on the reader of Psalms and Proverbs, Ecclesiastes (The Teacher) is a welcome interlude. In my first reading of the whole Bible, this is the book that made the greatest impression on me. For those who are searching, it has an explosive starting chapter.   "Utterly   meaningless!   Everything   is meaningless" (1.2); it rapidly moves to "there is nothing new under the sun" (1.9); and concludes "For with much wisdom comes much sorrow, the more knowledge, the more grief" (1.18). Within seconds, the writer had my attention, sympathy and respect.

I wanted the writer to be King Solomon. It is so much easier to believe in someone with great accomplishments. When such a person says everything is "chasing after the wind" (2.11), I listen. The futility of this phrase made a deep impact on me; it is an important part of this book and is mentioned five times (2.17, 4.4, 4.6, 4.16, 6.9). Like the wind, its effects increase with repetition.

Equally, the practical advice rings true: "A man can do nothing better than to eat and drink and find satisfaction in his work" (2.24). Slightly modified this is repeated four times (3.13, 3.22, 5.18, 8.15). In a Bible of much "do" and "do not", it was hard to understand why this particular advice stood out. On reflection, I believe it was because it was a complete formula for living and it was much more practical than to "love".

Ecclesiastes is the one book in the Bible that I have read

over 50 times. I am a gambler and I believe in chance so it is not surprising that I can relate to "There is a time for everything" (3.1) or "no man knows whether love or hate awaits him" (9.1). I also found justification for work: "The sleep of the labourer is sweet" (5.12); and "A good name is better than fine perfume" (7.1). And when things went wrong "Sorrow is better than laughter" (7.2) or "righteous men get what the wicked deserve and wicked men get what the righteous deserve" (8.14).

One recurring question I ask myself is : why bother to work and study? The answer was clear: "wisdom is a shelter as money is a shelter" (7.12). And the end of the Ecclesiastes says it all: "For God will bring every deed into judgement, including every hidden thing whether it is good or evil" (12.14).

Conclusion

My reading of the whole Bible had taught me much. It had required great discipline and I could easily see why so few people complete the task. Modern life has too many distractions; many nights I had to "sacrifice" reading the newspapers or watching television to do my Bible reading. There were many parts of the Bible that were a joy to read. I understood so much more. Yet, there was so much I forgot, and there was a lot I had to read and re-read. It was like my gap-year: great activity, much done, but nearly impossible to answer the question – what did you learn? I did not find a plan to live my religion. I had a long way to go.

CHAPTER THREE

THE BIBLE BACKWARDS

I finished reading the whole Bible on 21st August 1996. It had taken nearly 19 months. What had I learned? I had expected to have the "knowledge" and to be able to speak with authority on the whole book. Sadly, it did not happen. Instead, my predominant feeling was of confusion and of information overload. It seemed that most of my insights were in the Old Testament. Was this simply because of how I had read the Bible? It was possible as I had read the Old Testament first, I had come away with that imprinted in my mind. On this evidence, I decided to read the Bible backwards! This was not as extreme as it might appear: I was only going to read the books of the Bible from the last to the first. I read each book in the normal way.

1.   James

In my second reading of the Bible, this book had the greatest impact on me. It was short (5 chapters) and to the point. Although some have described this book as a diatribe or not very well outlined, I loved its direct advice. It appeared to me that the author was more accustomed to preaching than writing, and I wondered if this work of James was originally a sermon.

The start is hard-hitting: "Consider it pure joy whenever you face trials of many kinds" (1.2). This was a man who believed in Christians being tested; this was not an easy, comfortable Christianity. But with trials and temptations, Christians were to pray: "If any of you lacks wisdom, he should ask God" (1.5). This approach to life will bring happiness and fulfilment: "Blessed is the man who perseveres under trial, because when he has stood the test, he will receive the crown of life that God has promised to those who love him" (1.12).

The next section was the most important in my second reading. It seemed to have had greater effect the second time. A nerve was touched by the question: "What good is it if a man claims to have faith but has no deeds?" (2.17). The answer was powerful: "Show me your faith without deeds and I will show you my faith by what I do" (2.18). Perhaps because of my upbringing or my personal circumstances, these words were like an electric shock of truth. My unhappiness with the behaviour of the Church seemed to be exonerated, and reinforced by "As the body without the spirit is dead, so faith without deeds is dead" (2.26).

James was probably the brother of Jesus, but it was his clarification of a few issues which impressed me. Sometimes I have felt that there was too much of an emphasis on the avoidance of evil so I welcomed the emphasis on doing good: "Anyone who knows the good he ought to do and doesn't do it, sins" (4.17). On reflection, I found James to be a mirror image of Ecclesiastes. In Ecclesiastes, the practical things (eating, drinking, joy in work) lead to faith; in James faith leads to the doing of good deeds. These two books are still my favourites in the Bible.

23

2.   Forgiveness

I have always been disturbed by how "love" pervades the New Testament. I am much happier with covenants and punishment. When Jesus says "love your enemies, do good to those who hate you" (Luke 6.27), I am unable to comply. On a good day I could do the second part of the quotation but I am not built to love my enemies.

As I examined my predicament, I wondered if I should approach my problem in a step wise way. While I had problems with "love", I did not with "forgiveness". When Jesus was faced with a paralytic man, he said "your sins are forgiven" (Mark 2.5) as he perceived that the man's greatest need was for forgiveness of his sins. Indeed, John the Baptist preached "a baptism of repentance for the forgiveness of sins" (Mark 1.4). I realised that I had most problems with "loving" my enemies as they did not show repentance. Jesus was crucified so that our sins would be forgiven. He did not wait for our repentance.

Jesus was able to say "Father, forgive them for they do not know what they are doing" (Luke 23.34). This has been a very useful verse for me. I can say this, in my heart, to my enemies. It allows me not to need their repentance. I feel that this is an improvement as, in the past, my first instinct would be to get my own back: "without the shedding of blood there is no forgiveness" (Hebrews 9.22). I do not know if I shall ever be able to love my enemies. Yet, I now allow myself the opportunities to admire them... and not to have the out and out total hatred of them.

A very great help has been my leaving my enemies to God.   Judgement and punishment is in His hands. However, I needed to stop myself taking action.   To this end, I am greatly helped by Psalm 70.1-2:

"Hasten , O God to save me;
O Lord, come quickly to help me.
May those who seek my life,
be put to shame and confusion;
may all who desire my ruin
be turned back in disgrace".

3.   Organisation

When I read of Jesus feeding 5,000 people (Matthew 14.13-21), I immediately thought of how he managed to organise such an event.   I am an organiser and I am easily distracted into the practicalities of a party rather than thinking of the people I might invite.   In my experience, it can be relatively easy to stimulate early enthusiasm, but to maintain and build an organisation may be more difficult.   Indeed, my problems have often been with ministers and congregations rather than with teaching.

I was heartened by the high qualifications required of overseers (bishops, 1 Timothy 3.2-6) who "must also have a good reputation with outsiders so that he will not fall into disgrace and into the devil's trap" (1 Timothy 3.7). Equally high qualifications are required of deacons and their wives (1 Timothy 3.8-12) and elders (Titus 1.6-9). The characteristics of the groups within the Church are considered, especially how to relate to them (1 Timothy 5.1-24) and teach them (Titus 2.1-15).

The problems in the organisation of the church do not seem to be in the Biblical advice, but that the people chosen do not appear to have the qualifications required of them. With intakes in Theological Colleges rapidly declining, matters may get worse.

Today, as in the past, there is a problem of false teaching. It is apparent to all if a large organisation has good principles and practice. The early church had these problems: "meaningless talk" (1 Timothy 1.6) and "they want to be teachers but they do not know what they are talking about" (1 Timothy 1.7). The problem is repeated in Titus: there are "mere talkers and deceivers" (Titus 1.10); and "They claim to know God but by their actions they deny him" (Titus 1.16). The Bible was clear in the advice for the church about people who caused problems: "Warn a divisive person once, and then warn him a second time. After that, have nothing to do with him" (Titus 3.10). It is a great pity that this advice is rarely acted upon.

The life recommended for the organisation was simple: "if we have food and clothing, we will be content with that" (1 Timothy 6.8). The warning "For the love of money is a root of all kinds of evil" (1 Timothy 6.10) is perhaps even more relevant today. What can be said to be the mission statement of the organisation also has great appeal:
"Our people must learn to devote themselves to doing what is good, in order that they may provide for daily necessities and not live unproductive lives" (Titus 3.14).

4.   Suffering

Modern man feels that he can avoid suffering. They do not want infections when they should recognise infections are necessary to stimulate the immune system. I believe that some of the problem lies in the perception of Jesus, who says "I lay down my life for the sheep" (John 10.15). So, Jesus does the suffering and the sheep carry on as before.

The people of the Old Testament really understood suffering, and the need to voice their complaints. The books of Job, Lamentations and some of Psalms are great examples of this necessary dialogue with God. God understands and expects this reaction: "when he cries out to me, I will hear" (Exodus 22.27). However, suffering can be a punishment: "those who sow trouble reap it" (Job 4.8).   More than this, subsequent generations suffer for the sins of some: "he punishes the children and their children for the sin of the fathers to the third and fourth generations" (Exodus 34.7).

There are two great benefits of suffering: education and the test of faith. I have always regarded the relationship between a father and son as the closest to that of God and myself. The words "My son, do not despise the Lord's discipline and do not resent his rebuke, because the Lord disciplines those he loves, as a father the son he delights in" (Proverbs 3.11-12) are the words that I know I feel with my sons. And sometimes the lesson is difficult and you have to say: "If after all this you will not listen to me, I will punish you for your sins seven times over" (Leviticus 26.18). Then, as every parent knows the warning can be ignored and you are faced with the decision of what to do next. Here, God gives the perfect example: "I myself will be hostile towards you and will afflict you for your sins seven times over" (Leviticus 26.24).

Suffering can also be a test of faith: "When he has tested me, I shall come forth as gold" (Job 23.10). In modern society, this is even more misunderstood. People not only expect not to suffer, but also not to have their faith tested. The current, politically correct position is that life must be easy and everybody must pass the exam. This is unreal. Life is about learning and this is often about blood, sweat and tears. The politically correct often do more harm than good.

Jesus showed the way: "If they persecute me, they will persecute you also" (John 15.20). Thus, suffering is part of every Christian's life: the cross is about suffering for all, not only Jesus. But Jesus has shown us the way and it is easier to follow his example: "You should follow in his steps" (1 Peter 2.21). The position adopted by Paul is the ideal: "We also rejoice in our sufferings, because we know that suffering produces perseverance; perseverance, character; and character, hope. And hope does not disappoint us, because God has poured out his love into our hearts" (Romans 5.3-5).

Conclusion

My reading of the Bible backwards was different. I was guilty of skimming the 'boring' bits, and focussing on important verses that I had underlined on my first reading. Familiarity was breeding contempt. However, I also knew that I had to spend a lot of time with difficult verses as all was not going 'to be revealed later'. Although I finished my second reading faster, I spent greater quality time with important sections in the Bible.

I knew that I had regarded the whole Bible as one book. I had not considered the range of authorship, historical context or genre. Already I had information overload and greater study would have provided even more data to be analysed and assessed. My approach was simplistic but it was all that I could manage. The second reading of the Bible provided me with lots of new information that I had missed on my first reading. However, I was no nearer having a simple plan of action.

CHAPTER FOUR

IMPORTANT MESSAGES

After my second reading of the Bible, I had begun to focus on important messages. As a scientist, I felt that the Bible had too much data for most Christians to read and remember. Indeed, I wondered how many Christians could be expected to read the whole Bible. If it could not be expected of all, then what was the purpose of the Bible? I concluded that the Bible had to cover all situations, so help and advice could usually be obtained. It was therefore necessary to have only a working knowledge of the whole Bible. For each person, more detailed study would be required of parts of the Bible dependent on their own requirements.

The question remained of how one could identify these important messages? My readings had identified some key messages, but were these the important ones? I decided that I probably should see what other people felt to be important. Thus, I started another quest of reading what others had written on the Bible.

1.   Sermons

"The Times: Best sermons of 1996" is an enterprising book: from more than 200 entrants, 31 sermons are published from The Times "Preacher of the Year" award. Several denominations are represented but most were Anglican. The book was edited by Ruth Gledhill and even though a sermon should be heard, these read very well indeed.

I love sermons - they are the part of the Christian Church service that I most enjoy. As in past times, I would go a long way for a good sermon. This book does not disappoint. Sermons covered current events such as the Dunblane massacre and the consequences of Human Immunodeficiency Virus infection, as well as perennial problems of society such as marriage and divorce, put into a modern context. However, it was a perceptive sermon by John Thompson called "Everyone did as they pleased" which had the greatest effect; it showed how little observance there is of the ten commandments and that the position is analogous to that in the book of Judges.

In all these sermons there was humour. This was welcomed as it is not a feature of the Bible even though humour is a great teacher. One candidate, Ian Knox, said he loved the tombstone which read "Here lies a lawyer and Christian" which prompts the question as to why two people were buried in one grave. This was a great introduction to a lawyer's perspective on the Good Samaritan. Another candidate, John Cook, had an introduction that said the book of Jonah "may be the best known in all the Bible and also the least understood"; he got my attention, but his argument that the "story is a very big joke" was unconvincing. I recognised that humour is individual and perhaps too much so for the Bible.

Predictably, there were good sermons for important days:

Passion Sunday, Lent, Remembrance Sunday and Christmas. However, the messages on trust and perseverance had more effect. It was inspirational of Graham Rogerson to use the "Mastermind" television programme phrase "I've started so I shall finish" to illustrate perseverance. There were 62% of quotations from the New Testament although the Bible is 77% Old Testament. These sermons reflected my experience that sermons today are disproportionately quoting the New Testament. Yet, it was a pleasant surprise that the sermon that most impressed me was based on Exodus 20.8, "the seventh day is a Sabbath to the Lord, your God. On it you shall not do any work". I knew this commandment well, but I was not prepared for David Heywood's comments: the Sabbath is "the gift of rest"; "Rest is not optional, it is God's command"; and "Rest is discipline". My reading of these sermons had reinforced my important messages and made them more relevant. It was enjoyable and as I read one a day, I could feel I had had seven Sundays each week.

2.   More sermons

I was satisfied with myself and quickly bought "The Times: Best Sermons for 1998". It was so much easier to read a sermon than the Bible; the preacher is trying to stimulate you whereas the Bible can sometimes be a test of dedication and perseverance. I was also expecting a sermon to give me a greater insight to what was said in the Bible; sermons were by teachers and I was a student. As sermons can be described as the inspired word of God, my approach appeared justified. My self-satisfaction could not be higher.

As I read on, disappointment grew and grew. In the first book of sermons, by my assessment 2/31 (6%) were very average; but in this book, the number had grown to 13/30 (43%). As with the first book, quotations were centred on the New Testament, and there was the same proportion as before. One new factor was that 3 sermons did not have a teaching text. In addition, there were five sermons on important days, and two on the Lord's Prayer. Overall, I felt that there was a dumbing down in the sermons with poorer teaching.

I like to have my imagination stimulated by the sermon and to be taught. It was nice to be reminded that a "tabernacle" is a "tent" so the church is a large tent. Joyce Critchlow's sermon "Salt is good" was very educational: salt being used on flat house roofs to keep the house cool in summer and warm in winter; and bakers use salt in their ovens to increase combustion. The comparison of salt and faith was superb, and, I greatly enjoyed this sermon – it should have won!

For me, one runner-up would have been Macheny Shafer's sermon on eating. He observed that the Bible mentions meals or eating over 860 times. A central part of Jesus' ministry took place over a meal, and he appears to his disciples after his resurrection for a hot meal on the beach. This sermon had great insights as did my second runner-up sermon by Lorna Sivyour on faith and fear. This sermon was very well argued and at the end I totally believed that there is "a two-sided coin, one side is fear and one is faith".

In the first book of sermons, there were only 10% female;

in the second there were 43%. My disappointment in the second book was in the teaching and detail. Could this be due to the female approach to sermons? Not so, the 3 sermons without specific Bible quotations were by men; and, of my top 3 sermons, 2 were by women. I read these two books over two months and at the end, I recognised that I had to move on from sermons – they were no easy answer to my quest.

3.   Firm foundations

I have also been a great believer in having good foundations. After the butterfly journey with the Best Sermons series, I was glad to find a little book "Firm Foundations" by Peter Jeffery and Owen Milton. This book was first published in 1981, second edition in 1987 and reprinted in 1993. The objective of the book was to provide daily readings from great chapters of the Bible; there were 62 readings. My approach was as with my readings of the Bible and the Best Sermons series. I was looking for daily readings in which I learnt or found a new insight. Inevitably, my choices are individual. Not only was I influenced by my previous knowledge and experience but a lot depended on my mood and tiredness. My readings were done late at night after a long day and a night's work; if I had had a bad day, it would take a lot to impress me. This was perhaps unfair to some readings, but this was not a controlled experiment and it was the overall impression of the entire book which was important.

The Psalms were 11% of this book but only 7% of the Bible. Psalm 1 apparently shows us "very clearly the difference between the Christian and everyone else". I felt that this statement was economical with the facts: as this was Old Testament, it showed the difference between Jews (as well as Christians) and everyone else. There was a worse example of inaccuracy in this book. After quoting "He will baptise you with the Holy Spirit and with fire" (Matthew 3.11), it is noted that fire is mentioned 400 times in the Old Testament and 70 times in the New Testament. Then there is this: "In 1665 the Great Plague swept through London. Out of the population of 450,000 people, 60,000 died of cholera. Men were powerless to stop this terrible march of death. Then, came the Great Fire of London". The implication is that the Great Fire stopped the Great Plague which was cholera. The Great Plague was not cholera (which is due to Vibrio cholerae) but is caused by Yersinia pestis, a totally different bacterium. While cholera is a food or waterborne infection, plague is spread by rats and so fire may have stopped the spread of plague by killing rats, but cholera would be unaffected.

The other psalms were more impressive. Psalm 23 was described as holding "a place in the heart of Christians unrivalled by almost any other portion of Scripture". It was more important that this Psalm focussed on what God was doing for Christians and His ever presence. It was fitting that Psalm 73 was chosen to show that the godly frequently suffer and the ungodly often prosper. This Psalm finishes with a recognition that envy is sinful and that it is better to be near to God than have other riches. The third psalm was Psalm 103 which is described as "the Everest of the Psalms" as it does not have a prayer or petition but is filled with praise for God.

35

This book seemed to have a similar mix of Old Testament (40%) to New Testament (60%) as the Best Sermons. Interestingly, I was impressed by only 18/62 (29%) chapters: there were an equal amount of Old and New Testament chapters. It appeared that my study had made it more difficult to be impressed by teaching. Was I becoming indifferent because of familiarity?

"Lost and found" was a smart description of Luke Chapter 15. It described 3 kinds of being lost: naturally (like sheep), helplessly (like the coin) and wilfully (like the son). All of these situations have various degrees of "blame" yet Jesus saves them all – it was beautifully argued. My delight in this chapter was somewhat worrying: I liked clever interpretation. Nevertheless I felt that the word should be enough. In 1 Peter 2, the Word of God ("pure spiritual milk") is all that we should need. I should be happy to belong to God ("a stone" v8) and recognise "to suffer unjustly is a remarkable opportunity of glorifying God". This chapter closed with a quotation from F. B. Meyer "The sheep cannot expect to fare better than the Shepherd".

Of the 62 chapters, one made a tremendous effect on me. It was "The Call of God" (1 Samuel 3). I had read this chapter in the Bible twice before but it had not been memorable. Now it was, why? First, the scene was set: priests were corrupt, Eli was very weak and "The word of the Lord was rare". Secondly, God called Samuel three times and each time the call was clear but Samuel thought it was Eli; the comment "Thank God for his infinite patience with us!" struck home. Lastly, when Eli realises what is happening, the comment was very perceptive "others can see the Lord dealing with us before we ourselves are aware of it".

Conclusion

I had hoped that my training as a scientist would allow me to develop a plan to bring God into my daily life. This had not happened. I had approached the problem as I would a scientific one: collecting data, assessing it and deciding on the next step. I had enjoyed reading others' important messages. I had learnt a lot. It seemed that I was collecting a lot of wonderful data, but after 3 years I had hoped to be further on. The objective of having a plan was as elusive as ever. I was becoming depressed with my task and beginning to wonder if I had better join a group that would give me a pre-digested answer to my problems. I quickly rejected this fantasy. As a scientist I had always enjoyed finding a different path. It was time to critically assess my position.

CHAPTER FIVE

PAUL

My position did not appear good. I was doing a lot of reading and getting a lot of learning, but it all seemed to mean less and less. I had tried reading the Bible and others' interpretation of what was important. I had believed that if I could adopt a scientific approach to the problem, that I could make real progress. The truth was I was making little progress. Why?

I took a couple of weeks to ponder my position. With science, I had learnt over the years that action without careful consideration is often unproductive. And whenever I was confused (as I was now), it was critical to identify an important principle that could be explored and tested. After 2 weeks, I concluded that my study was too broad (the whole Bible) and that my subjects (God, Jesus, etc) were too large. Therefore, I needed a smaller subject and one area of the Bible. For a week, I considered more detailed study of Moses, Samuel, Job, John, Peter and Paul. I recognise that many would have a quite different list to consider, but at the time, these were the names that came to mind. One of my sons would have chosen Job. However, after much reflection, I felt that I should study Paul in greater detail.

1.   Paul the Man

I chose Paul for very many reasons, but most of all I like

38

the story of Paul. He was described as "a man of little stature, thin-haired upon the head, crooked in the legs" (White, 1989). In contrast, the description "in person he is unimpressive and his speaking amounts to nothing" (2 Corinthians 10.10) seems praise. Yet, this man had an impressive curriculum vitae: "five times flogged, three times beaten with rods, once stoned, three times shipwrecked, 24 hours adrift at sea, in continual danger from rivers, robbers, his own people, Gentiles, in the city, in the wilderness, at sea and from false brethren; in toil and hardship, through many a sleepless night, in hunger and thirst often without food, in cold and exposure" (White, 1989). This was no natural hero, but there is no doubt that his achievements were heroic.

Paul started life as a Jew and a Pharisee; not just a Pharisee, but a Shammaite Pharisee –"one of the strictest of the strict" (Wright, 1997). This was a man who always had strong principles and discipline. Paul was also a Roman citizen and a Greek speaker; Wilson (1997) comments: "It would be hard to exaggerate the importance of Paul being a Greek speaker". Greek was the real language of the Empire and being a Roman citizen made travel very much easier for Paul. The man therefore had the necessary characteristics of an evangelist.

While Paul was persecuting Christians (Acts 22.3-5), on the road near Damascus, "Suddenly a bright light from heaven flashed around me" (Acts 22.6). He was blinded and was subsequently told "The God of our fathers has chosen you" (Acts 22.14). The fact that Paul was not one of the Apostles chosen by Jesus in his lifetime endeared him to me. He did not have the evidence of personal experience as the other Apostles. Yet, Paul's experience was life-changing: God "was pleased to reveal his son to me" (Galatians 1.16) and "Have I not seen Jesus our Lord?" (1 Corinthians 9.1). I would like to think that some may have similar revelations, but perhaps not as intense and complete.

Paul took pride in "we work hard with our own hands" (1 Corinthians 4.12). "He was a tentmaker" (Acts 18.3) and used his skill to support himself and did not rely on charity. It transpires that for Jews tent making "was a questionable activity for the devout" (Wilson 1997). This was because tanning leather, even though it was not produced from pigs was forbidden to Jews. I liked Paul's financial independence – it made me feel that this was a man you could trust.

2.   A writer of letters

Paul's writing is nearly a quarter of the New Testament and just a little less than Luke's. Many have studied Paul's work with the latest technology and analysis, and questioned whether Paul wrote Hebrews (White, 1989; Wilson, 1997), 2 Thessalonians and Ephesians (Wilson, 1997). There is also the consideration that writings may have been lost. Perhaps more important is the realisation that "it was not considered dishonest in the ancient world to write something and then attribute it to the pen of someone you greatly admired" (Wilson, 1997). Paul also used secretaries and this can create further problems as I have found to my own cost. While Mark's is probably the oldest Gospel, Paul's work may antedate

40

Mark's by 20 years (Wilson, 1997) and has the position of the oldest Christian document.

I must admit that I enjoyed reading more about Paul (Bruce, 1977; Clements, 1994; Sanders, 1991). Over the months, I moved away from thinking of the small details to the wider picture. I began to see Paul as a father writing to his offspring. At this time, I was writing weekly letters to my sons at University and I appreciated one great factor in Paul's writing – the needs of the recipients governed the content and approach of each letter. I could not match Paul's experience, range of advice nor certainty, but, I could admire his professionalism and recognise that my admiration grew with study. I felt that when Paul was asked what was his occupation, the reply should have been not "tentmaker" but "writer of letters".

As a "father", Paul knew that he had to warn his readers about divisions in the church, its causes and wrong conceptions (1 Corinthians Chs 1-4). False teaching was always present, and Christians needed to guard against this and reject it (Colossians 2.8-23). Warnings against these dangers had to be reinforced by rules for holy living (Colossians 3.1-17; 1 Thessalonians 4.1-12). When Paul was being attacked by false teachers, he was quick to defend himself: explaining his conduct and ministry (2 Corinthians Chs 1-7) and vindicating his Apostolic authority (2 Corinthians Chs 10-13).

"Thank you" letters are always difficult to write. When one is imprisoned gifts are much more appreciated, and Paul's letter to the Philippians reflect this position. This letter is an example of one in which teaching was secondary and there are no Old Testament quotations.

Yet, as a father, he encourages his readers to stand firm against persecution (1.27-29), and then "Do not be anxious about anything" (4.6). Paul also finishes by reassuring his readers that "I have learned to be content whatever the circumstances" (4.11). I found this letter a good format for "thank you" letters.

In contrast to the Philippians' letter, his letter to the Galatians expresses his unhappiness. He gets to the point: "I am astonished." (1.6) and "You foolish Galatians!" (3.1) There is also a simple course: "let him be eternally condemned" (1.8). However it is Paul's discussion of justification by faith which is memorable. This book in the Bible has been called "Martin Luther's book" as he has used this as a basis for his teaching, in particular "know that a man is not justified by observing the law, but by faith in Jesus Christ" (2.16). Paul still encourages the doing of good (6.1-10): test "his own actions" (6.4), "carry his own load" (6.5) and concludes with "A man reaps what he sows" (6.7). Finally, Paul finishes by showing that circumcision is not necessary for Christians (6.12-16). This is a letter with remarkable emotion and content.

As a true writer of letters, Paul has a full range within letters and of types of letters. Within 1 Corinthians, he has the most popular chapter on love (Ch 13) and the most unpopular on worship (Ch 11). There are the letters of recommendation: the whole of Philemon to win the acceptance of Onesimus; and in Romans when he recommends Phoebe (16.1). However, it is in Romans where there is a masterpiece of an "application" for a job. Paul writes this letter to prepare for his visit to Rome, and to obtain Roman finances for his missionary trip to Spain. There is the easy start followed by the hard-hitting presentation of learning with Old Testament quotations (Chs 9-11); then there is righteousness in the world and among Christians (Chs 12-15), with emphasis on the relationship between Jew and Gentile in God's plan (14.1-6). You can see why he got the job.

3.   Resurrection

Paul deals with this subject in an expert way. Apparently, he "inherited the belief in a coming resurrection of the body which was widespread among the Pharisees" (Bruce, 1977).   Nevertheless he had to deal with important questions from the early Church.   Some had felt that they had already received the new life and Paul had to mock them with "you really had become kings" (1 Corinthians 4.8). Paul's belief was a different life: "he who raised Christ from the dead will also give life to your mortal bodies" (Romans 8.11).

Some ministers and senior church members feel that it is acceptable not to believe in the resurrection.   I totally disagree. Paul said: "If there is no resurrection of the dead, then not even Christ has been raised" (1 Corinthians 15.13). And the full implication of this is that "if Christ has not been raised, our preaching is useless and so is your faith" (1 Corinthians 15.4). The logic is excellent, but how can our learned members of the Church still expect to be paid for their unbelief?

The Thessalonians wondered what would happen to those who had already died. Paul was clear: "we who are still alive and are left until the coming of the Lord will certainly not precede those who have fallen asleep" (1 Thessalonians 4.15). This was interesting as it moved away from the Jewish idea of resurrection of everyone at the same time to that of the Greek concept of individual immortality.

Paul is not precise on when the Lord will come; but, recognises it will not be expected "like a thief in the night" (1 Thessalonians 5.2). Paul describes the process: "we who are still alive and are left will be caught up together with them in the clouds to meet the Lord in the air" (1 Thessalonians 4.17). This description is not found in the Gospels.

He also recognises that there will be a difference: "the dead will be raised imperishable, and we will be changed" (1 Corinthians 15.52). This change will mean that there will not be the same human form but "the likeness of the man from heaven" (1 Corinthians 15.49). Paul understood death; I Thessalonians 4.13-18 are the most quoted at funeral services. White (1989) goes further: "Paul's six verses have brought strong comfort and hope to millions of hearts at Christian funeral services".

Conclusion

Paul was an exceptional man. He is easy to admire for his accomplishments and for what he says. There is the voice of experience and knowledge. Yet, he says so much that it is difficult to come away with a plan of action. I know that I could spend several years studying Paul's writings and still have much to learn. I recognise that other authors have analysed Paul's character in great detail and that I have probably not done him justice. Nevertheless, this chapter recounts the profound effect that some of Paul's writings had on me and I have not tried to make a balanced assessment of Paul's life or all of his writings.

To follow Paul would require drastic changes in my life. One could argue that this was what was required, however, I have always believed that if something was right with a drastic change, it would also be right with a small change. My quest was for incremental change and I needed somewhere to start.

CHAPTER SIX

JOY/PRAYER

Throughout my quest, I had firmly believed that my 30 years in scientific research would give me a great advantage. Now, I was beginning to wonder if it was a disadvantage. I had focussed on collecting data: I now had lots of data, insights but no plan of action. It is always difficult when you start to believe that your whole approach may be wrong. At these times, my experience in science had taught me it was important to trust your 'gut' reactions and instincts. Despite all the negative results, I believed deep-down, that my approach was fundamentally correct.

As my mood was low, I suddenly decided one rainy Sunday afternoon to focus on JOY. I had always liked C. S. Lewis "Surprised by Joy" – the title was tremendous and evoked many promises. This book described the author's conversion from an atheist to a Christian. He concludes by saying that joy "has lost all interest for me since I became a Christian". His analogy was that like someone of a lost party seeing the first signpost in the woods. The whole party gathers around and stares. However as the party see signposts every few miles, there is a loss of interest. This was not my position on joy. I could not identify with C. S. Lewis; it did not ring true for me.

1.   Joy

My position on joy was that it reflected the relationship with God: "You will fill me with joy in your presence" (Psalms 16.11). It was the word that heralded Jesus' arrival in the world. The angels had "good news of great joy" (Luke 2.10). And during his life, there was "Jesus full of joy through the Holy Spirit" (Luke 10.2). Joy was an emotion to be treasured: it represented the relationship with God in the Old Testament, and Jesus in the New Testament.

I found a gem of a little book called "Meditations on Joy" by Sister Wendy Beckett (1995). This book focuses on the spiritual power of great art, and is obviously a book written by someone who has spent many years in contemplation. She describes joy "as profoundly right', as what 'ought to be'" And then there is a wonderful sentence: "It may be the weaker spirits who, for their faith, need the encouragement of joy; saints can live in the bare reality of joy, without the need actually to feel its wonder" I was a weaker spirit and did need the encouragement of joy.

I then remembered: "For the Kingdom of God is … joy in the Holy Spirit" (Romans 14.17). After the death of Jesus, the joy was through the Holy Spirit. And this was reinforced with the experiences of the disciples. "And the disciples were filled with joy and with the Holy Spirit" (Acts 13.52). I had noticed that a recurring theme of Paul in his books was his mentioning of praying in the first chapter. I had liked this good solid practice. One verse that I had doubly underlined was: "I always pray with Joy"

(Phillipians 1.4). This linkage of prayer and joy was a step forward. It made sense and provided a means through which the Holy Spirit could act. Yet, to be able to "always" pray with joy seemed impossible. I had looked upon joy as something that was occasional and not "always". What do I mean by "prayer"? The New Collins Concise English Dictionary defines prayer as "personal communication or petition addressed to a deity". This I felt was a good starting point.

My deliberations returned me to Sister Beckett (1995). She states: "Joy is prayer experienced, or to put it another way, joy gives us the bliss of actually feeling the reality into which prayer can draw us. We see truth in joy, receive it in prayer". These words had great wisdom, and yet again I wondered how this book of few words could be so profound. Now, my position had become: joy was reflected by the relationship with God enabled through prayer.

2.   Mechanics of prayer

As I contemplated my insight on joy and prayer, I came across another book with a great title: "Illuminata: thoughts, prayers, rites of passage" by Marianne Williamson (1994). She says prayer is a "ladder to God" and "prayer is God's greatest gift to us". There are other memorable quotes: "Prayer gives us the strength to endure, the tools to make miracles" and "The purpose of prayer is to bring Heaven and earth together". However, I was looking for the practical mechanics of prayer: "a comfortable, private place; silence... a commitment to making spiritual practice a part of our lives". And "we must spend as much time as we can give each morning". As you would expect, this book is packed full of wonderful prayers for all occasions. There are too many to quote, and many hidden treasures.

I am a practical man. And I was now preoccupied with the detail of praying. I returned to Bonds (1979) and the chapter "Great men of prayer". This was a bit frightening: "Mr Wesley spent two hours daily in prayer. He began at four in the morning"; "John Fletcher stained the walls of his room by the breath of his prayers"; Luther said: "If I fail to spend two hours in prayer each morning, the devil gets the victory through the day"; and "Payson wore the hard-wood boards into grooves where his knees pressed so often and so long". From these great men, it seems that a minimum of two hours of prayer a day was acceptable. Williamson (1994) believed "as much time as we can". Yet, this seemed far too much and I was daunted by the discipline required for such practice.

Bonds (1979) had more demands: "The men who have done the most for God in this world have been early on their knees". An early morning prayer session seemed essential as God had to be first in our thoughts. But what of sleep? The answer was simple: "A desire for God which cannot break the chains of sleep is a weak thing". I started to regret my search for the mechanics of prayer as I now felt that it was almost impossible to do what was required.

Jesus' advice on prayer: "go into your room, close the door and pray to your father"; "do not keep on babbling like pagans"; and then there is the Lord's prayer

(Matthew 6.6-13). I had always liked the Lord's prayer and it had given me great comfort, but this would not take two hours. Yet, Jesus was known to pray for longer periods: "Jesus went out to a mountainside to pray, and spent the night praying to God" (Luke 6.12). I was confused. Two difficulties appeared: how long was one to pray and what one should say to God.

3. Continuous prayer

I had always liked small books: they are easy to carry and the message is usually not too complicated. It is the explanation of why I do not buy 'blockbusters' – they are big and complicated. I also like to get the message quickly – I do not want to read a thousand pages to get to the point. On a long trip, I bought a little book: 'One-minute Pocket Bible' by Mike Murdock (1984). This book had had an impressive pedigree – third printing and over 50,000 books in print. I liked many of the topics in the book, but was drawn to 'Prayer'. The conclusion for the topic was profound "One hour in the presence of God will reveal any flaw in your most carefully laid plans". However, one quotation stood out like a beacon: "Pray without ceasing" (1 Thessalonians 5.17). How had I missed this quotation?

Had I been reading too quickly? I returned to "Power through prayer" (Bonds 1979), and looked for this quotation. I did not find it. Instead, on page 107, I found that the apostles should give themselves "continually to prayer" (Acts 6.4). However when I looked at this quotation in my Bible, I found that the apostles should "give our attention to prayer". "Give attention" does not have the full impact of "continually"; and both words are very weak compared to "without ceasing". What was the correct translation? Somehow it did not matter. What was more important is that I had found this quotation. I had missed it in all of my reading because of the different use of words and translations. This was an important lesson. Obviously, for me, certain words trigger further study and investigation; and others I happily read quickly. Now, that I had found the quotation, I had to consider long and hard what it meant.

Weeks passed and I made little progress. My mind wandered. I was having a difficult time at work and I returned to reading "Ecclesiastes". This was my comfort book, and I never tire of reading it. It also makes me stop and think. Months later, I started reading "Dare to Journey with Henri Nouwen" by Charles Ringma (1992). Dr Ringma believes that our "religious institutions often fail to aid us in our spiritual development"; and his book emphasises the 'how' of the development of the spiritual life.

Reflection 42 in this book (Ringma, 1992) is 1 Thessalonians 5.17 and the reflection is called: "The prayer of the heart: a way of persevering". This reflection looks on prayer as a "state of being". It can take on many forms but "its abiding characteristic is that it is with us whether we consciously pray, work, eat or sleep". This was heavy stuff but lacked detail – how could it be with us at all of these times? This is not answered. And the statement "It is a prayer that is maintained not by an act of the will, but by our very being" was not very helpful. There were important unanswered questions: How did you know if you had reached this stage? How could you reach this stage? The comment that the prayer of the heart is sometimes as basic as: "Please God, don't let me go" was even more confusing. Why was this "basic"? How did you pray after "basic"? I did not feel that Dr Ringma had given me the "how". My quest had to go on.

4.   Joy in prayer

"The Last word" by Wallace Benn (1996) examines the last days of Jesus and finishes with a chapter on "Christian Joy". This starts with a wonderful quotation: "Joy is faith dancing: peace is faith resting". However, there was much more: there is joy in knowledge; joy in obedience; and joy in prayer. This latter section seemed to bring together a lot of what I had been struggling to understand.

There is the quotation: "Until now you have not asked for anything in my name. Ask and you will receive, and your joy will be complete" (John 16.24). This is interpreted as: "God does want us to pray specifically in order that we may have the joy of seeing him work in answer to our prayers". I did not totally agree with this interpretation. But I was happy with the further explanation: "Sometimes God says 'No' as well as 'Yes' or 'Not yet'". The further discussion that many requests would have been disasters if God had granted than was excellent.

This chapter then states that "Christians pray on average for one minute a day" and pastors "about one minute and thirty seconds". With this information I could not understand "there is joy in prayer, and there will be a corresponding lack of joy when we do not pray". Why did people and pastors not want more joy in their lives? The final statement: "The most joyful churches are the praying churches!" was difficult to understand. Did not all churches have a duty to pray? Why was prayer a "take it" or "leave it"? If there was joy in prayer, then, there could be a limitation for each person, was this why no one more than 1-1 ½ minutes. It did not quite make sense.

5.   Conclusion

My studies had confirmed the relationship of joy and prayer. From my basic definition of prayer as "personal communication or petition addressed to a deity", I had developed a greater understanding of prayer. However, the mechanics of prayer to achieve joy were a major stumbling block. I had several important insights, but still worried about how long one should pray and what one should say to God. The suggestion that there should be continuous prayer seemed to raise more problems than it resolved. Yet, throughout this time, I became more convinced than ever that there was joy in prayer. Although there were many unanswered questions on the technicalities, it seemed more and more that this area of my study was both "right" and "basic".

CHAPTER SEVEN

HOW AND WHAT

I had expected that I might have answered the question "How to pray?" at a different time from "What to say to God?" I was wrong. I answered both these questions at the same time. It was a hot, sunny day in London. The atmosphere was humid and dusty. I was tired. I was about to go home when I decided to quickly look at some books. In among the shelves, I saw an innocent looking book.

I still do not know why I picked it up. The cover was simple and unremarkable. I believe that nine times out of ten I would have briefly looked at the cover and put the book back, but somehow I was drawn to open the book and read more. The book was "The Way of a Pilgrim" translated by Olga Savin (1996). The foreword by Father Thomas Hopko records that the origin of this work is a mystery. We follow the story of the pilgrim without knowing if he existed, but the book reminds us that "we are all pilgrims on a journey to God". And Father Hopko concludes by saying the book "provides protection and nourishment for the trip". For me, it was more. It answered my most important questions, and provided the basis of my plan to live out my religious beliefs.

1.   Was it by chance?

Was it by chance that I found this book? On the first

page, the first Biblical quotation was – 1 Thessalonians 5.17, "Pray without ceasing". I was amazed that this verse was the subject of the book. More interesting was that this verse had had the same effect on the author as myself. He said "I began to wonder how one could pray without ceasing". His next questions were also mine: "What should I do?" and "Where will I find someone who would be able to explain this to me?".

Like the author, I asked Christians and ministers. Their answers were: "It is not meant to be taken literally"; "It is just an ideal"; "If you lived in a monastery, this is what you would do"; and "It is a translation difficulty, it really means you must think of God a lot." The author received a better answer "Unceasing interior prayer is the continual striving of man's spirit towards God". But, it was not sufficient, it did not provide enough detail.

The author's journey continued and "in several different places, I also encountered this same divine instruction". But real answers were few and I sympathised with one conclusion "very rarely does one obtain any substantial answers from present-day preachers". My journey seemed so similar to the author from centuries ago. I had empathy with each experience even though he appeared to make better progress than I.

Then, he found a staret (a monk distinguished for his saintliness). This man knew things. This man gave real answers; and it was no longer a philosophical/theological explanation. Instead, the author was told what was the prayer to be used for unceasing prayer. But more, the staret gave the author a book called "Philokalia" in which

25 holy Fathers teach unceasing prayer. It was marvellous! At last, I had answers which made sense. Now, many years later, I still wonder if I had found this book by chance. My whole approach to prayer and practice was dramatically changed by this book. If I had not found this book, I am sure that the years that followed would have been quite different. This book gave me a direction, and I do not believe that I found it by chance.

2.   One answer

The author's staret said that the words for unceasing prayer were "Lord Jesus Christ, have mercy on me!" This was the prayer to be said either "with your lips or only in your mind". It was one answer – a very good one. But what was it like in practice? The author (Savin, 1996) practised the prayer for one week in a quiet place sitting alone and in silence. There was initial progress but then "a great heaviness, laziness, boredom and drowsiness began to overcome me, while a mass of thoughts clouded my mind". I realised that praying was not going to be easy even if you had the prayer.

The author's staret was not surprised. His answer was: "That, beloved brother, is the kingdom of darkness waging war against you".   The staret's advice was perseverance, and the author "in the solitude of my hut, I repeated the Jesus prayer six thousand times a day". Quite amazingly; it helped the author. Surely, the staret would be pleased, but not so.   He now advised persevering and strengthening the habit. The author was "to repeat the prayer, without fail, twelve thousand times a day". This meant that the author had to rise earlier and sleep later. Amazingly, the author took only two days to do as he was told, although his "tongue became numb and jaws felt stiff". The good news of finding the prayer was rapidly being overshadowed by the impracticality of living a normal life. The author was happy to live in solitude as a watchman for a kitchen garden. His work allowed him to behave as he did, but this was not something everybody could do. Could one only become close to God by living alone or in a monastery? This could not be my answer as most people do not live like this. I concluded that it was only easier to be close to God in these circumstances. The average person needed a different strategy.

3.   More techniques

Although I was starting to feel disillusioned, I persisted. There was the useful technique of synchronising the prayer with your breathing. As you breathe in, you say "Lord Jesus Christ"; and then as you breathe out: "have mercy on me". This worked well and after many hours, one seemed to be praying as you breathe.

The refinement of the technique was as taught by Saint Gregory of Sinai - the prayer was repeated as the mind visualised the beats of the heart. After many months the author found that the "mind and heart began to act and recite the prayer without any effort". At this stage, the author was living in isolation on a diet of bread and water.

He spent all of his time on the Jesus prayer and it brought him everything. When he was "bitterly cold", he would pray more fervently and soon he would be "warm all over". When he was "hungry", "ill" or in "pain" – the Jesus prayer resolved his problems. It even protected him against wild animals. As I read, I practised the Jesus prayer. This was a very difficult time for me, and I got into the habit of saying the Jesus prayer hundreds of times during the day. This brought peace to my mind; and it was very comforting. I started to believe that if I reached 12,000 times in a day, great things could happen. But I never did. My life had too many distractions.

4. Final questions

There were two questions which required answers: Is the Jesus prayer the right prayer? And is repetition of this prayer what is meant by "unceasing" or "continuous"? To the first question, "Lord Jesus Christ have mercy on me" is not a verse in the Bible. There are many quotations on the theme: "Have mercy on me, O God" (Psalms 57.1); "Lord God Almighty will have mercy" (Amos 5.15); "I will have mercy on whom I have mercy" (Romans 5.15); and "I will do whatever you ask in my name" (John 14.13). It is clear that God can have mercy and it is reasonable for us to pray for mercy. But this prayer is not in the Bible. When I repeated this to a minister, I was accused of being too pedantic. For most, there is enough in the Bible for this to be a reasonable, acceptable prayer.

The second question is equally difficult to answer. When Jesus gave advice on prayer it was the Lord's Prayer (Matthew 6.9-13). So, should not continuous prayer be the Lord's Prayer? Jesus also warned against "babbling" (Matthew 6.7) – was the Jesus prayer babbling?

These questions occupied me for many months. Finally I came to several conclusions. First, the Jesus prayer was not "babbling"; indeed, it required total concentration and commitment. Second, although the Jesus prayer is not in the Bible, there are sufficient other quotations to make it "authentic". I even consoled myself that much of what Jesus said is lost and maybe he said something similar. Lastly, I was influenced by the quotation: "to live a recollected interior life, one must take any single passage from the Holy Scriptures, focus all one's attention and meditate on it, for as long as possible, and the light of understanding will be revealed. The same must happen with prayer" (Savin, 1996).

Conclusion

I was delighted to find "The Way of a Pilgrim" (Savin, 1996). It seemed to give me practical, direct answers of how and what I should pray. It even offered some detailed techniques on how progress can be maintained. And I did make progress; I found great peace. Then, I started to have questions. These questions were small compared to the overall benefit of the insights in this book, but they had to be addressed. In the end, I still regarded this book as a great find. My belief was now that this book could provide a core to my plan. However, there was a need for refinement and development. I still did not have a plan that was liveable in the modern world. I needed a plan that did not require the individual to become a recluse.

59

CHAPTER EIGHT

OUR LIVES TODAY

Many feel that their lives are full. In the developed world, there is work, responsibilities and perceived lifestyles. Bills, taxes and the mortgage have to be paid; the family looked after; and some time found for enjoyment of life. There is little time for religion. If one goes to church on Sunday, it is above average, and "enough" in our modern world. My quest has been to find how I could do more – how I could live out my religious beliefs. So far, I had made progress in understanding continuous prayer; however, I recognised that there needed to be refinements to this practice to adapt to our lives now.

The next insight was from "The Wounded Stag" by William Johnston (1984). In this book, an Irish Jesuit compares "Christian mysticism with its Buddhist counterpart". This is a learned book and introduced me to two subjects: the desert fathers and the presence of God. I will discuss these subjects in separate chapters later; however, here it was like having a very, very hot chilli, my senses were rudely awakened and brought to life.

1.   Commitment

The title "The Wounded Stag" was from a quotation from St John of the Cross: "The wounded stag appears on the hill". Johnston (1984) equates the stag to Jesus. A characteristic of a wounded stag is "to climb to high places" and "to race in search of refreshment and cool water". The author chose this symbol "because it shows that all Christian mysticism has its origin not in our love for Jesus but in the mystery of his great love for us". Johnston (1984) concludes that the stag "is wounded with compassion; he is wounded with love".

Johnston (1984) tackles the subject of mysticism and peace. Why is the world in conflict? Jesus said "Blessed are the peacemakers for they shall be called the children of God" (Matthew 5.9). There also needs to be a commitment to peace and rejection of violence: "Gandhi said powerfully that the violent person knows how to die". Bravely, the author considers the "Irish Conflict", and states "Mysticism means loving the gospel, living the gospel and allowing ourselves to be transformed by the gospel". This leads on to "As today there is no living Christianity without a living commitment to peace, so there is no mystical Christianity without a mystical commitment to peace".

This book concludes with "I argue that the only answer to the agony of Ulster is a total and radical commitment to the gospel on the part of a significant number of people on both sides of the border". Sadly, the gospel can be interpreted differently by different groups. However, the final thought was valid: "And then I realised anew that the problems of Ireland are the problems of the world".

2.   A holy man

We have always admired holy men. The Beatles made it

popular to have a guru. And today, we have moved to the psychiatrist, counsellor or confidante; however, these are not "holy" men. The problem is that the newspapers are full of the misdeeds of holy men so that we do not know whom to believe. In this position, I came across "The Holy Man's Journey" by Susan Trott (1998). I liked the way this book is laid out, and soon I was captivated by the content. It is about a holy man who journeys to see his sick teacher.

The holy man is Joe who was "like a rock: steady and safe". He is different from other holy men because "I am not a man so much as an idea". He is sick yet recognises that "he has become successful, even famous, through talent, discipline and perseverance, the three main qualities for achievement". Yet, he knows that there is more that makes us unique: generosity, failure, laziness, fearlessness and compassion. Joe chooses Anna to go on his journey; she was "meant to be with him at this time of his life".

I like Joe. He "admires people who go too far". And says "I am an old man, I've fulfilled my years. The real pain of loss is when the person is young". This is what I know. I love being old as it gives me freedom to say what I feel. Also I believe that "the day of death is better than the day of birth" (Ecclesiastes 7.1). One is very fortunate to have had years to live and make mistakes.

Joe and Anna leave the hermitage and venture into the outside world. Here, Joe has to interact with people they meet. He is able to excel. He has concepts: "Always leave them laughing"; "They survive not by being helped by each other but by helping each other"; and "Taking the blame, even if you didn't do it, smoothes the knottiest situation spectacularly and immediately". Joe's journey to his teacher is completed, but Anna is not impressed by Joe's teacher, Chen: "Despite his charismatic presence, her clouded feelings about him were not dispelled". His lavish lifestyle and fleet of cars did not help. Not Joe, he was happy. For Anna, "Distrust prevailed, and every time she looked at Joe's glowing face, she felt mystified".

Joe dies. Anna does not understand: Joe was sick, yet he journeyed to be near his teacher who was supposed to be sick. Chen understood: "He honoured me with his death" Anna realises that she has to succeed Joe. Everyone else including Chen, learnt from Joe's death. Joe had "left the world a better place". He was a true holy man, but this enjoyable book is fiction. I want to believe in people like Joe, but I tend to see only fakes. Lastly, I ponder that maybe true holy men are "one in ten thousand million". They exist, can be seen, but are very rare.

3.   The Toronto Blessing

In January 1994, in the Airport Vineyard church in Toronto something happened which some felt was a major outpouring of the Holy Spirit. This "Toronto Blessing" spread from this little church to the whole world. Was it the work of God or the Devil? I decided that I needed a good assessment of the situation. Although there are many books on this subject, I tried to find one that looked most objective. The book I chose was Mike Fearon's (1994): "A breath of fresh air". At the time this book was written the Blessing had reached many hundreds of Britain's churches and thousands worldwide.

Fearon (1994) has two persuasive assessments: first, whether the Toronto Blessing is of the Holy Spirit, and second is if the Toronto Blessing is responsible for the 1994 phenomenon in British churches. For the first assessment, Fearon identifies false teaching: there is "no biblical basis for anyone receiving a 'double portion' of the Holy Spirit"; "wealth as a natural consequence of following Christ"; and "God would make them richer if they were generous givers". On this background, could the Holy Spirit still be present? Fearon's answer is: "The simple test is root and fruit: ask where is it coming from and where is it heading?" The answers are not good: the roots appear "in a person hungry for the sensational"; and there are "blossom and not fruit". The assessment was that the "The Blessing is only good if it equips people to move out into society", and it did not. The conclusion is that "the manifestations appear to be contrary to God's perceived word in the Scriptures".

Apparently, "The Blessing was spreading across the USA like wildfire several months before the outbreak in Toronto". In Britain, much was happening in Pentecostal and Charismatic churches. There was a spirit of renewal and as in the USA, a "phenomenal hunger for the Lord, expressed in worship". Fearon (1994) concludes that the phenomena in British churches "have little to do with the Toronto Airport Vineyard – that connection appears to have been a convenient media story – but even the word "blessing" (singular) is inappropriate". There were a host of different blessings. Nevertheless, Fearon (1994) also suggests that "the 1994 'wave' will fuel the renewal movement, but it's too early to judge whether the whole Church will be affected".

Conclusion

Our lives today appear full, but yet there is an emptiness. To fill that emptiness, we can turn to holy men or more direct experience of the Holy Spirit in phenomena such as the Toronto Blessing. There appears to be a real hunger for such experiences in modern society. I, being a teacher also, was attracted to the idea of someone or some church giving me an enlightening experience. However, this attractiveness was reduced by the recognition that holy men are rare, and the Toronto Blessing is probably a media concept. There are many undercurrents in our lives today and there is little that is straightforward. Perhaps what was required to solve our problems was the individual commitment of each of us. The test was the fruit. As I looked at my life, I asked the simple question: what was the fruit? was there only blossom?

CHAPTER NINE

PRESENCE OF GOD

I had an hour to waste before my train departed, and I decided to browse in a bookshop. It was raining and I was looking for something to lift my mood. The first book I picked up did the job. In the introduction, the author wrote "I was looking, absurd as that may sound, for small books". I love small books, and I had not recognised that there were others who like me felt "Books had to be little ones". The author (Blaiklock, 1981) was a young man "seeking to integrate faith, life and learning". He found a little green book by "a cook from a Carmelite monastery kitchen who seemed without effort to turn the haunting last words of Christ into the simplicities of common living". The book was "The Practice of the Presence of God" by Brother Lawrence, and I had found Blaiklock's English translation.

1.   Brother Lawrence

Brother Lawrence was a Carmelite monk who died in 1691. The translation by Blaiklock (1981) records how Brother Lawrence "in his monastery kitchen discovered an overwhelming delight in God's presence". I recalled Jesus' words "Remain in me, and I will remain in you. No branch can bear fruit by itself; it must remain on the vine. Neither can you bear fruit unless you remain in me" (John 15.4). "Remain" in some translations is "Abide"; both are powerful statements: "Remain in me" or "Abide in me".

From the start, it is clear that Brother Lawrence was an unusual man. He was converted at 18 years old when he saw a tree stripped of its leaves in winter and reflected "That after a time its leaves would appear again and then flowers and fruits, he received a lofty view of the providence and power of God". How many of us would have this reaction to trees stripped of leaves in the winter? The more common reaction would be: "it is winter – a depressing cold time of year!" As high as his opinion is of God, his opinion of himself was low and he describes himself as "a big heavy-handed fellow who broke everything".

As he saw his weaknesses his answer was to enter the monastery. But he did not expect to find peace or God's love. Instead, he expected suffering. He felt that "he would be made to smart for his acts of clumsiness and mistakes". One is not surprised that a man with this attitude found contentment in the monastery. Also, one sees how unusual Brother Lawrence was in that he then says that God had disappointed him as he had found contentment. More than that, he frequently feels that his life is too easy and is forced to say to God "You have deceived me".

2.   Conversations and letters

There are four conversations; three take place in 1666 and one in 1667. In his first conversation, Brother Lawrence's philosophy is revealed: he believes that we should "fix ourselves firmly in the presence of God by conversing all the time with him". Immediately I recognised this as a variant of "Pray continually" (1

Thessalonians 5.17). However, there was also a development of the Pauline quotation: "conversing all the time" with God allowed us "to fix ourselves firmly in the presence of God". I had not considered that prayer/conversation "fixed" myself in God's presence. Instead, I had assumed that God was always listening. My concept therefore changed from God being like a "Big Brother" on a television/video link to my standing/kneeling before him. This new concept made everything more direct and personal.

Apparently Brother Lawrence had a "natural aversion" to working in the kitchen. However, instead of asking to be moved, he "trained himself to do everything there for the love of God". He was so successful that he spent 15 years in the kitchen. His method was simple, but at least he recognised that things did not just happen. Instead, "a little perseverance was needed at first to form the habit of conversing all the time with God". Brother Lawrence is a deceptive man: he appears to keep things simple, but he also has enormous insight. This is illustrated in: "It was enormous self-deception to believe that the time of prayer must be different from any other". I had to read this passage several times. He is right. Yet, the majority of the world looks upon prayer as quite different from normal living. This man was living his religion and had much to teach me.

I like to believe that I am a scientist and so analysis of results is what I like to do. Brother Lawrence is very interesting because he is an experiment. His life demonstrates what can be achieved. He is a result. It is because of this that I liked this advice: "He found in God what was needful to be done at the present moment". It seemed that a concept of continual presence of God allowed Brother Lawrence to live his beliefs. This was confirmed by "He had reached the point where he thought only of God". A great positive result.

The sixteen letters take 25% more space than the conversations. The written word can be very different from the spoken with Brother Lawrence. He restates his position: "I do nothing else but abide in his holy presence". However, he also adds valuable detail on the process. First "I know that the heart must be empty of all else". And one needed to welcome God by saying "My God, here I am, all yours", or "Lord, fashion me according to thy heart". These details are very useful, as is the observation "the smallest remembrance will always please him".

As in the conversations, several characteristics stood out. Brother Lawrence was a humble man: "I regard myself as the most wretched of all men". He had a logical mind: "But how can we be with him without thinking of him?" Yet, the simple message is still present: "To live as if there were none but he and I in the world". How many of us could take our beliefs to this level? But perhaps only if we can, can we hope to reach: "When we are this preoccupied with God, sufferings will be only times of happiness, balm and consolation". Brother Lawrence turns everything on its head, he looks forward to the happiness of suffering and wonders why God does not make him suffer more! I began to feel that I would not have liked to meet Brother Lawrence as all of my arguments would be seen as simplistic.

4. Principles and practices

The second half of the book explains the principles and practices essential to acquire a spiritual life. Much of this section repeats what has already been said. We must "during all our labour and in all else we do…. pause for some short moment, as often indeed as we can, to worship God in spirit and truth"; have "purity of life"; and show "faithfulness" in the practice of the presence of God. Brother Lawrence had assumed that others had these prerequisites, however, they were not essential to start the practice of the presence of God. I looked upon it like learning to swim: lots of things need to come together at the same time, but several could be learnt at the same time.

I did not learn to swim until I was 18 years old. It was a traumatic experience and I am still surprised that I managed to learn. Similarly, the practice of the presence of God was not easy.   Even Brother Lawrence "confessed that it was hard at the outset and that there were many times when he would forget his exercise". This reassured me. But I was also encouraged that the practice "far from distracting him from his work, enabled him to do well". This was a compelling reason to adopt these practices.

I tried adopting the practice of the presence of God. It was fine for an instant, but then I would rapidly return to reality. It was therefore comforting that Brother Lawrence also had several experiences of the practice: "sometimes a hazy vision of him or a diffuse long gaze"; "a remembering of God"; and "an alertness towards God, a wordless conversation with him". These further descriptions allowed me to appreciate the complexity of the practice. I had a long way to go before I could develop "a clear and distinct knowledge of God". But there were very good reasons to persevere.

Conclusion

Brother Lawrence died when he was eighty years old. It must have been wonderful to be able to say that the practice of the presence of God had the great benefits of "I no longer believe, I see and experience". For me, the practice reinforced continuous prayer. I had focussed on repetition of prayer, but after reading Brother Lawrence, I created an environment for my prayer. I now visualised myself before God as I repeated my prayer.

CHAPTER TEN

DESERT FATHERS

Brother Lawrence's life was a stimulus for me to think about monasteries. Was it easier to follow God in a monastery? I found myself thinking about this question more and more. Superficially, the answer should be "Yes". However, a lot must depend on the monastery, its rules and the community; and I could see that some communities could be worse than living in the outside world. I was confused. But how did it start? For many months, I did not have any answers to these two questions. Then, one day as I was looking for a book on prayer, I saw the title "Heaven Begins Within You" by Anselm Gruen (1999). The title was not the reason that I picked the book; the reason was the picture of desert sands and the subtitle "wisdom from the desert fathers". I saw no relationship between the title and subtitle: I had much to learn.

1.   A little wisdom

From the introduction to this book, I learnt that around 300 AD "the first signs of the monastic movement began to appear. At first, men were drawn to places of solitude and then to the desert". Although the "Bible itself issues no call to monastic life", monasticism was common to many religions. "Stabilitas" means staying by oneself or remaining in the community that one has entered. St Benedict saw this stability to be the antidote to constant

72

movement and migration. He used the analogy of a tree which needed to remain in one place to develop roots and grow; constant movement prevented growth. Within the community, the monk spent most of the time in his "kellion" or cell. Monks were forever singing the praises of the cell. The cell was an infirmary and heaven: a place of healing and where one could sense God's loving.

The desert was believed to be the dwelling place of demons. The desert was the place where Jesus was tempted. Father Anthony believed that in "the desert was the place where the demons showed themselves more clearly and undisguisedly". The monks had to prove themselves by dealing with temptation and triumphing over the demons. But it was not a single battle, it was continuous: "Temptation keeps the monks awake and makes them continue growing within". Constant temptation was necessary and so the retreat to the desert was not to avoid temptations of the city. Instead, the desert allowed one to deal with one's own sins. "Without temptation, the monks became careless".

I had always believed that the ascetic was "someone who practices great self-denial and abstains from worldly comforts and pleasures", and this is how the New Collins Concise English dictionary defines the word. I was delighted to learn that "ascetism actually means exercising so as to obtain a skill". The skill is to overcome your passions. According to Father Evagruis this means "perfect fasting, powerful deeds, humility, scarcely disturbed or completely undisturbed silence, and unbroken prayer".

Control of the body was important. The monks did not eat meat and some ate only every other day. However, exaggerated fasting was to be avoided. Excessive sleep was discouraged and fatigue was a "prerequisite for experiencing God intensively". The night was when "God visits humans and speaks to their hearts". It was critical that ascetism was preparation for receiving God's grace – God alone can work our salvation.

The monks had a structured day. Father Pambo's day was fasting until evening, silence and a great deal of manual labour. After meeting others, Father John would on arrival home take time for "prayer, meditation and psalm-singing until his thoughts were restored to an orderly state". External order brought the monks internal order. This healthy way of living made the soul healthy. I easily identified with the principles of the desert fathers. I read Anselm Gruen's book (1999) many times; it is packed with wisdom. I was glad to be introduced to early Christian monastic traditions. I was amazed at how mankind was still asking the same questions.

2. More wisdom

My search to find out more about the desert fathers was quickly satisfied. I found "The Word in the Desert" by Douglas Burton-Christie (1993). This is a large book of 336 pages and small type. I usually do not buy such books, however, it passed my large book test. I opened the book at random three times and read one page each time. The writing was excellent all three times and I was enthralled. I bought the book and spent the next three months reading it.

The monks in the desert were accused of being antisocial, anti-cultural and unbiblical. Many had retreated into the desert because of financial, social or personal disasters. Not unlike the Crusader Knights many centuries later, they were privileged and educated. They were not of the lower social classes. Thus, the accusation probably did have some validity. However, the test would be what was achieved in the desert. There were insights on the Biblical texts: a recognition that "we not only read the text, but are read by it"; and that prayer adds "to the understanding of the texts and the texts feeding and deepening the experience of prayer". The desert fathers were not unbiblical but biblical as "words were expressed in lives". An assessment of what was achieved by the desert fathers, a realisation of their influence on contemporary thought and the relevance of their approach even in the modern day does not equate with accusations of antisocial or anti-cultural behaviour.

The monks found freedom from their past in the desert. But there were other freedoms: from anxiety, attachments to possessions and ego. There was also space to enjoy the presence of God, to love others and enjoy the simple life. Their lives reflected their religious beliefs: "do not worry about your life" (Matthew 6.25); "do not store up for yourselves treasures on earth" (Matthew 6.19); and "love your enemies" (Matthew 5.43). However, the linchpin of their lives was a total dependence on God: "cast your cares on the Lord" (Psalm 55.22).

There is a great deal more that I could write about

75

Burton-Christie's book (1993). However, for me, the most important benefits gained were in understanding the environment in which "continuous prayer" was acted upon. The early monks had the Bible's word as a central role in their lives. Their lifestyles allowed them to live their religious beliefs. My reading made me realise how simple it all could be, but also, how difficult it was to put into practice.

3. Mount Athos

I have spent many holidays in Greece and love the country and way of life. For years, I have been fascinated by Mount Athos, the Holy Mountain. So, it was with very little hesitation that I purchased "Athos, travels on the Holy Mountain" by Matthew Spencer (2000). In the twentieth century, the Greek government granted the peninsula of Athos the status of "Semi-autonomous republic". The monasteries on Athos are able to regulate travel to and from their territory, levy their own taxes and make their own laws. Thus, "women, female domestic animals and beardless youths" are excluded and it is difficult for anyone to gain a visa to visit. Athos has twenty main monasteries but there are also other communities and hermitages. All were trying to follow God in their own way.

I could see that in the first few centuries AD monastic life may have been attractive as there were not many alternatives. But today, seminaries are empty and modern men are not attracted to the ministry. What relevance would the monastic life of Athos have to offer today? Monastic life is disciplined with the monks rising at 4 am for Matins. There are eight hours of work during the day emphasised by Paul's letter to the Thessalonians: "If a man will not work, he shall not eat" (2 Thessalonians 3.10). But at mid-morning, noon and late afternoon there are breaks for individual prayer. The brothers assemble for prayers to finish the day, and go to bed very early. The day has routine and ritual. This discipline is an essential part of monastic life.

I like a daily routine. My ideal is to arise early and to go to bed early. I also love food. The diet of the pilgrim (Savin, 1996) of bread and water would be too strict for me. On Mount Athos, there is a great emphasis on food. However, Mondays, Wednesdays and Fridays are fast days when the monks do not eat until the evening. On fast days there are nuts and honey, but otherwise bread and olives with some "very oily dishes". On the non-fast days, lunch has dishes of "oil drenched okra, lentils, peppers, rice and bowls of salad over which, for good measure, you are expected to pour a good dose of even more olive oil".

I am a meat-eater. Yet if vegetarian meals are properly prepared and tasty, I enjoy them. Thus, I love many Chinese and Indian meals that have no meat. However, I have a particular fondness for good olive oil. Thus, although Spencer (2000) was unhappy to swim his food in olive oil, I love this custom. Then, the knack is to use the lovely Greek bread to mop up all of the food-flavoured olive oil. My love of olive oil started decades ago when I admired olive trees that were in barren landscape but were hundreds of years old. I figured that any tree that could live centuries must have secrets.

Now, I treat myself to cook only with extra virgin olive oil. Spencer's (2000) experiences of those living on Athos echoed the writings on the desert fathers (Gruen,1999; Burton-Christie, 1993). Today's monks still have much in common with the monks of yesterday. These men were not escaping from the world, but had changed their priorities. Within the monastery, they were able to establish the routines and rituals which would bring them closer to God. As in the outside world where the rules to success were well established; in the monastery, one could not become close to God unless one had triumphed over one's inner demons.

Conclusion

I loved many of the routines and rituals of monastic life. I liked that the spiritual component of life is not an optional, add-on extra, but gives life its meaning. However, I did not feel that it would be easier to follow God in a monastery. Now, I wanted routines and rituals that allowed me to live in the turmoil of the modern world. I did not want to renounce my family life, friends and work, but wanted my religious beliefs to be integrated into that life. As I read more of early Christianity, I recognised that I wanted to stay within the Judeo-Christian framework. This was my upbringing and here I was comfortable. The months reading about monastic life were not wasted, I learnt that perhaps for some, the monastic life would be suitable. However, for me, I had to find different solutions.

CHAPTER ELEVEN

STEPS BACKWARDS

As a scientist, I know that there are periods of rapid progress and then everything could go into reverse when someone asks a simple question. I had been making good progress. A deeper understanding of continuous prayer and the presence of God were solid foundations. However, the rejection of monastic life as a solution to my own problems increased the reliance on myself. So far, I had accepted the words in the Bible without question. Indeed, I was so pleased with myself at having read the Bible that I did not question its validity. In science, the wrong path is often taken because of initial, incorrect assumptions. Suddenly, I felt that I should have asked more questions instead of being pleased by my performance. This was not a good time.

1. Are they reliable?

I spent a month trying to decide what to do and visiting bookshops and libraries. I prayed and I wished that I could ask a "guru" or "staret". But I have always been a lonely scientist: I was always in the covered wagon rather than in the band wagon. In my search to live my religious beliefs, I wanted to adopt the same practices as in my scientific life. I trusted that God would lead me to the right path. Yet, I was very pleasantly relieved when I found "The New Testament Documents – Are they reliable?" by F.F. Bruce (2000). This book has an impressive pedigree. It was first published in 1943 and the 2000 printing was the sixth edition. F.F. Bruce was Rylands Professor of Biblical Criticism and Exegesis at the University of Manchester.

Bruce (2000) examines the evidence for the 27 books of the New Testament with special consideration of the Gospels, Acts and writings of Paul. The arguments for the validity of the New Testament are compelling. Bruce (2000) tells that the evidence for the New Testament amounts to some 5000 Greek manuscripts with the best around AD 350; whereas, for other writings of the same era, for example, Caesar's "Gallic Wars" (written between 58-50 BC) there are about 9 good manuscripts and the oldest written around AD 850. He also argues if Jesus' resurrection did not happen, why did the Romans (or others) not produce evidence against the event? It would have been the best way to stop the story being told.

I learnt that the feeding of the multitudes were not duplicate accounts. The feeding of the 5000 (men, not counting women and children) with 5 loaves and two fishes is recorded in all of the Gospels (Matthew 14.15; Mark 6.35; Luke 9.13; John 6.1). However, the feeding of 4000 (men, not counting women and children) with 7 loaves and a few fishes is only recorded in two Gospels (Matthew 15.32; Mark 8.1). I learnt that one feeding was on Jewish soil for Jews (the 5000) and the other (the 4000) on Gentile soil for Gentiles. They demonstrated that "Christ was bread of life for Gentiles and Jews". Also, "the bread represents the harvest of the land, the fish will represent the harvest of the sea".

## 2.	Hidden sayings of Jesus

One of the tricks of scientists is to have little bits of work which need to be done but are not done immediately. These are known as dotting the "i"s and crossing the "t"s. Often, these jobs may not be regarded as very important, but when done can give a greater insight to the main work. Such was the case in "Hidden Sayings of Jesus" by William Morrice (1997). This book examines the sayings of Jesus that are not recorded in the four Gospels. There were many books left out of the 27 books included in the New Testament as we know it, especially important was the Gospel of Thomas.

The Gospel of Thomas begins "These are the hidden sayings which the living Jesus spoke and Didymus Judas Thomas wrote". There is little or no narrative, but 114 composite sayings and 15 parables recorded by the author. This compares with 66 parallel sayings and 12 parables in the Gospels. I was immediately impressed by: "A prophet is not acceptable in his own country neither does a doctor work cures on those who know him", Thomas 31 (11.6). The first part of this quotation is found in Luke 4.24 and John 4.4. However, I found the expansion of the quotation allowed a greater understanding of the first part. It also is reflected in Luke 4.23: "Physician, heal yourself!".

There are three parables in the Gospel of Thomas that are not mentioned in the Bible. I particularly liked: "The Kingdom of the Father is like a woman who was carrying a jar full of meal. While she was walking on a distant road, the handle of the jar broke. The meal streamed out behind her on the road. She did not know it since she had not noticed the accident. After she came into the house, she put the jar down and found it empty". I agree that this parable is "a warning against Christian self-assurance and lack of watchfulness". I liked the emphasis that the Kingdom of God has analogies in the everyday, simple things we do.

I greatly enjoyed Morrice (1997) references to the Desert Fathers and the Pachomian Monasteries. I still am amazed at how the desert communities grew from "a few" to "5000", or how "50,000 monks would gather to celebrate Easter". All of my readings of Burton-Christie (1993) and Gruen (1999) were reinforced. Morrice (1997) found space in his book to recall the story of a group of philosophers who tried to bait the desert monk, Theodore. They said "You pride yourselves on knowing the scriptures as well as their interpretation. So now, tell us who was not born and died, who was born but did not die, who died but did not decay". Theodore answered: "Oh you whose mind is like a leaking barrel, dwindles like a breath and fades away! He who died not having been born was Adam; he who was born but did not die was Enoch; while the one who died and did not decay was Lot's wife turned into a pillar of salt for the seasoning of such insipid minds as yours that strut so stupidly". This was strong stuff and I have always found stories such as these to be very convincing.

3. Mother Julian of Norwich

In 1373, Mother Julian was a recluse in a church in Norwich. She received 16 visions; she was 30 years old and described as "a simple creature, unlettered". She was wise enough to realise "The Revelation itself does not make me good. I am only good if as a result I love God more". So, she spent the next 20 years pondering in prayer the significance of her 16 visions and educating herself. The result was the first book in the English language to be written by a woman. The 86 chapters are wonderful. "Revelations of Divine Love" by Mother Julian of Norwich (edited by H Blackhouse and R Pipe) is a very special book. It is a book to be read and re-read. The language is perfect and the wisdom timeless. The start was not straightforward. "She had asked for three gifts from God: to understand the Passion of Jesus; to suffer physically as a young woman of 30; and to have three wounds as a gift from God". These were not the usual requests of 30-year-old women. The wounds were also not predictable: "wound of true sorrow for sin, the wound of natural compassion, and the wound of unshakeable longing for God". This is not a simple book and there were many chapters that I had to re-read several times.

I had several real insights. I agreed that "prayer unites the soul to God", but I learnt "to focus on the goodness of God is the highest form of prayer". But, her method in prayer was more revealing: "it is gazing at the Creator and loving him that makes us think less highly of ourselves". However, it was her thoughts on sin which I pondered for several weeks. I could understand: "Sin is the sharpest lash with which any of God's chosen souls can be flogged". But, I had not appreciated: "I did not see sin itself. I believe that sin has no substance or reality and cannot be known except through the pain it causes". This was really, really special. It made wonderful sense to focus on the pain rather than the sin. I had always believed in hating the sin rather than the sinner; but now, it was the pain that was caused. For me, as a doctor, it made perfect sense.

Mother Julian, despite her vision, had the same problems of living that beset us all: "My own wretchedness, my indolence, and weakness made me dislike the hard slog of my lot in life". I immediately recalled "he who humbles himself will be exalted" (Luke 14.11). Sister Julian lived the life God wanted. But this patience must also be for life: "God rewards the man who waits patiently upon God's will and for God's time, and who does not lose patience but makes it stretch over a lifetime". When one achieves this state of mind and practice, then: "Suddenly you will be taken out of all your pain, all your sickness, all your distress and all your sadness". Again, I recalled: "The day of the Lord will come like a thief" (2 Peter 3.10).

I guess that I had expected this book to be different as it was based on visions of God. Yet, it seemed to reinforce what was in the Bible, but stated in a more personal way: "He did not say: You will not have a rough time, you will not be burdened, you will not have to face difficulties". More importantly, the position of faith remains unchanged: "For it seems to me that in this life God does not keep an extra supply of goodness that is higher than faith, and there is no help at all in anything that is below it. Within faith is where the Lord wants us to stay".

Conclusion

Many might feel that I accepted the validity of the Bible

too quickly. I considered only one author and only the Gospels. The validity of the remaining new testament and all of the old testament were not examined. For a lot of people, my approach would be totally inadequate, and I accept this criticism. Yet, I spent many months thinking, reflecting and assessing my feelings. In my scientific life, I have always followed my feelings and after 6 months, I believed the Bible to be valid even though I had not struggled with the nature of metaphor, symbolic language and interpretation of scripture. However, it was a scientific conviction and not a strong belief. It took Mother Julian for me to realise that I believed with my heart. Why was this? After great deliberations, I realised that it was because her visions did not give her wonderful advantages, but she still had to work and struggle with her faith. She had the problems I had; strangely, I was comforted.

CHAPTER TWELVE

CHOTKI, CHANTING AND CANDLES

I have always believed that theory and practice must go together closely. I was learning a lot of theory, but what of my practice? As to be expected, the practice was not as easy as I had envisaged. Somehow I felt that at my age, with my experience, it would be easy to incorporate what I was learning into practice. Like all learning, this was not the case; before I could make real progress, I needed some help, some secrets of the game, some crutches. All of my life, I have believed in the "secrets of the game". Yet, as I was considering my religious beliefs, I felt that my faith should be enough. It was humbling to realise that my faith could not move objects, and I needed all of the help that I could get. As a scientist, I knew that it was easy to read of an experiment in a scientific publication and not be able to repeat the experiment when one first tried. Often, it required 3-5 experiments before one learned the "tricks" or "secrets". My religious life was mirroring my scientific life.

1.   Chotki

I returned to Savin (1996) "The way of a Pilgrim" to find the chotki. The chotki is a rosary or prayer rope: "prayers said.   Sometimes also used for other prayers". Obviously, a prayer rope was not discreet or practical for my work. I decided to use wooden beads as I wanted something simple. I bought a bracelet of 21 rounded wooden beads for fifty pence. By notching the middle bead, I could keep the beads in my pocket, counting prayers of ten or twenty-one.

It worked beautifully. I could easily put my hand in my pocket and start to count my prayers. As I walked down the corridor, sat in a meeting or drinking coffee, I would rattle off twenty-one prayers. The chotki also encouraged me to pray more... to do another ten and then another twenty-one. Even at home, as I watched television or listened to the radio, it became compulsive to do more prayers. Before the use of the chotki, I struggled to do 800-1000 prayers a day. With the chotki, I easily managed 2,500-3,000.

After 3 weeks, I had a problem, the constant friction had destroyed the elasticated string. So, I changed to a piece of leather. After 4 weeks, I had the same result - the leather was worn through. I had a real problem. It took several weeks before I managed to resolve matters by using a fishing line: "Ultima", 70 lb line, 0.70 mm. This was wonderful stuff and despite the friction, it seemed to have no effect on the line after 2 months. I was very pleased. This did not last long. One Monday, a very difficult day, I found that I had lost my chotki. Despite retracing all my steps and searching for one hour, I could not find it. Over the months I had become very attached to my chotki. The beads had become worn with my constant counting, and I believed that my prayers had infused into the beads. Somehow I felt that the lost chotki would be of some benefit to whoever found it. I ceased to search for it. Instead, that evening I tied my chotki to more fishing line and then to a key ring placed in the straps for my belt in my trousers.

2.   Chanting

My younger son has a natural affinity to chanting: from the repetition of words to put himself to sleep, or deep humming to prevent himself being sea-sick after his older brother had been. These practical benefits were a result of instinctive behaviour as no one else in the family chants. I had always regarded chanting as "singing one's prayers" so I was pleased to learn more on the subject from "Chanting – discovering spirit in sound" by Gass and Brehony (1999). It appears that chanting is worldwide with common threads in Hindu, Christian, African, Buddhist, Islamic/Sufi, Jewish and Shamanic chants.

I was reassured by "Chanting is not 'singing' – it's about breath, about heart and about Spirit, and we all come fully equipped to participate". I had always regarded myself as tone deaf and never took part in singing. I was further reassured: "You don't need a lot of vocal technique to chant". Chanting is said to be "The breath made audible and learning to breathe well is the first step in learning to chant". The instructions on chanting were excellent. Also, I learnt about some popular chants. The Hindu "OM" is properly pronounced AUM (A like the 'a' in amen, U like the 'oo' in cool and M, a long vibrating 'mmmmm' sound on the lips). The Buddhist "Heart Sutra" chant: Ga-tay. Ga-tay. Pa-ra Ga-tay. Pa-ra Sam Ga-tay. Bod-hi. Swa-ha means "Gone. Gone. Gone

88

beyond. Gone beyond the beyond. Hail to the one who awakens".

There is a superb chapter on chanting and ritual. I agreed that "daily rituals help bring rhythm into lives too often filled with random chaos". The Benedictine monasteries were an example "where year after year, decade after decade, life flows by with each day unfolding in the same rhythm, the same rituals, and the same chants". At first, I found the easiest places to chant were in the shower or walking along a deserted beach. Then, I found it very helpful just before I went to sleep and in the car to and from work. Most of all, I found "the chant is important, but often it is the silence afterward that truly moves us".

Gass and Brehony (1999) also quote from the "Way of the Pilgrim" and suggest that the Pilgrim chants the Jesus prayer as he walks, eats, lies down and rises. As someone who has tried, it is almost impossible to do 4000 chants a day – never mind 12,000. I believe that the pilgrim started chanting but quickly moved to "a prayer in the heart". As I found, chanting was a good ritual for certain times of the day and allowed you to move more quickly to unceasing prayer of the heart.

3. Candles

As I spent my early childhood living in a place without electricity, I have always loved candles. As an adult, I liked candles, but became a bit obsessed with burning all of the wax. Several times I had bought wide candles that looked nice but the sides did not burn; these were pretty but not practical. However, in churches, candles belonged and looked sensational. In the Greek Orthodox church where the walls were stained by the candle smoke, there was a special aura.

In yoga (which means 'union'), there is a process called "tratak" where one gazes at the flame of a lighted candle while sitting in meditation (Proto, 1989). The object is not to stare but to observe with "soft" eyes how the candle flickers and burns. However, with "flame meditation" (Harp, 1997), the object is "in a darkened room, from ten or fifteen inches away, stare intently at a candle's flame for one or two minutes". Then, "abruptly blow that candle out, and close your eyes. Within a few seconds, you'll begin to see the image of the flame again, apparently projected onto the inside of your eyelids. Watch that image for as long as you can". Like the peace after chanting, the darkness can have special significance.

I was delighted when I found Lakeland Plastic tealights. These are small candles with the wick on a drawing pin that burn all of the wax and can last up to 8 hours. I also loved Lakeland Plastic floating candles which are smoke-free and burn for up to 4 ½ hours. At first, I had loads of tealights and floating candles in large bowls – they created a wonderful atmosphere, and are a great antidote for depression although they are also a significant fire risk.

Later I burned candles in threes, probably to represent the Trinity. I was amazed at how often one candle would be blown out or not light; I always wondered which of the Trinity was not present. For meditation and prayer, I found that one or three candles were ideal. Too many candles were a distraction: a sight to be enjoyed but not a stimulus to pray. I developed the habit of lighting one candle whenever I returned home: this symbolised my return to the reflective life. As I meditated and prayed, I lit three candles. I blew them all out when I went to bed.

Conclusion

The process of living my beliefs required that I have some external help. The chotki helped me to pray; the chanting helped me to focus; and the candles created the right atmosphere. As a scientist, I was accustomed to having help from a variety of sources: stopwatch, scales, pipettes or measuring cylinders. I looked upon my chotki, chanting and candles in the same way: tools to help me achieve my aim of living my beliefs. As with all changes that you build into your life, such as dieting or exercise, the more you do the more you can do. The more I prayed, the more I was able to pray. I was also beginning to recognise that these solutions were personal and individual. Many people might have felt that it was more reasonable to join a church or other group. Like my scientific life, I was working alone and not joining established groups.

CHAPTER THIRTEEN

PEOPLE TODAY

I had spent a lot of time studying the past. Those whom I admired had lived a long time ago. I started to wonder about people living today. How did they live their religious beliefs? What could I learn from their lives? As a scientist, I had often recognised that what would have been acceptable and possible several hundred years ago would not be now. Science has made great progress in the last 100 years: what was thought to be true 100 years ago may not be true now. But did this apply to religious beliefs? My experience was that it is now more difficult to live your beliefs, and throughout this book I have struggled to find ways to bring God into my daily life.

I wondered if others had been more successful than myself and what I could learn from them. I decided to exclude individuals who were leading reclusive lives. I wanted to learn from individuals who were part of the modern world, but who were adept at making space and time for God in their daily lives. At first I was apprehensive as so many of my past heroes had been found to be seriously flawed. In my youth, I had greatly admired President John F Kennedy and Elvis Presley. Sadly, as I learned more of their lives I became disillusioned and disappointed with their behaviour. Amazingly, my present quest was very different.

1.   Mother Teresa

There is so much written about Mother Teresa, it is hard to know where to begin. Benenate and Durepos (1997) "Mother Teresa – no greater love" is a good start. Mother Teresa was born in 1910 as Agnes Bojaxhill in Skopje, Macedonia.   In 1931 Sister Teresa served as a geography and history teacher at St Mary's School in Calcutta; she took her final vows in 1937 and continued teaching.   On September 10, 1946, "God calls her to serve the poor". In 1948, she started to serve the poor; "after 1949, I saw young women arriving one after another.   All of them had been students of mine".   If Mother Teresa had not taught for 17 years in Calcutta, would she have had any followers?   I believe that her years of teaching and the special place Indians have for teachers ensured that she would have followers. It is a wonderful example of how work has to be done in God's time.   In 1950, the order of Missionaries of Charity was authorised by Rome.

Mother Teresa was demanding of her nuns: "We delight in poor food… possess only three sets of habits made of coarse cloth, mend and patch them and refuse to have extra; enjoy walking in any shape and colour of shoes; bathe with just a bucket of water". From her approach to life, she could say "our works are our witness", when compared to other religious groups, she could also emphasise "We have no fasting. Our fasting is to eat the food as we get it". Many times the nuns did not have enough food, yet, she would say "We never have any surplus, but we have never lacked what we need".

There was a wonderful story that made me think for a long time. Mother Teresa found a child from the street who was very hungry and gave her some bread. The little girl started to eat crumb by crumb. Mother Teresa said: "Eat , eat the bread. You are hungry". But the girl looked at her and said: "I am afraid. When the bread will be finished, I will be hungry again". Another story was of the 9000 people who the convent feeds each day: one day they ran out of food, but later in the day a truck full of bread came to the convent (Benenate 1997). The Government gives the poor children at school a slice of bread and some milk each day; that day, the schools were closed and the bread went to Mother Teresa.

The wisdom of Mother Teresa comes from a devoted life. On prayer, she says: "Listen in silence, because if your heart is full of other things you cannot hear the voice of God" (Benenate and Durepos 1997). Of her convent, there is: "There are many congregations that spoil the rich; it is good to have one congregation in the name of the poor, to spoil the poor". (Benenate 1997). Also, from this latter book: "There are many people who can do big things, but there are very few people who will do the small things". Each day people (some eaten by worms or rats) are rescued from the streets so that they could die surrounded by love and care.

2. Dalai Lama

His Holiness the Dalai Lama won the Nobel Peace Prize in 1989. He is the spiritual leader of the Tibetan people and since the Chinese army invaded Tibet in 1959, he has been exiled in India. During his exile, he has travelled the world teaching Tibetan Buddhism and putting the case for the Chinese to leave Tibet. The Dalai Lama has written many books but I chose to read his book with Dr Howard Cutler, "The Art of Happiness" (1998). Dr Cutler is an American medical psychotherapist and this book records his conversations and observations of the Dalai Lama. With Dr Cutler's Western perspective, the Dalai Lama's Tibetan Buddhist principles are examined in relation to life's problems in the Western world. I have always admired the Dalai Lama and I hoped that this joint book may be more objective than one written solely by the Dalai Lama.

The Dalai Lama, like Nelson Mandela, is able to show great compassion to his enemies. This book discusses the purpose of life and its relationship to happiness. However, there are great insights into suffering, for example: "It is our suffering that is the most basic element that we share with others". Yet, it is the Dalai Lama's philosophy when dealing with problems that is difficult to fault: "It is more sensible to spend the energy focussing on the solution rather than worrying about the problem". And the development of this thesis: "If there is a solution to the problem, there is no need to worry. If there is no solution, there is no sense in worrying either". Good sense and practical advice permeate this book. However, I felt a particular empathy with his observation. "One must integrate the religious teachings into one's life, wherever one is, so one can use them as a source of inner strength". This has been the object of my quest and it was comforting to have it stated so simply.

As I had now come to expect, his comments on prayer

were predictable: "Prayer is, for the most part, a simple daily reminder of your deeply held principles and convictions". His further explanations reinforced what I had learnt with great difficulty: "In my daily practice, my own daily prayers, if I go leisurely, it takes about four hours". It was interesting that at the lecture where he made this statement, a housewife said "I'm a working mother with small children, with very little free time". The Dalai Lama replied: "Even in my case, if I wish to complain, I can always complain about lack of time". He then laughed and added: "You can sacrifice some of your fun, so at least, I think daily say half an hour". This was how I had started and then there developed an inner desire to pray more as "True spirituality is a mental attitude that you can practice at any time".

The great value of this book is that the Dalai Lama shows "his beliefs are not based on blind faith or religious dogma but rather on sound reasoning and direct experience". As a scientist I appreciated this approach to learning. I was also willing to accept the Dalai Lama's "belief that while attaining genuine and lasting happiness is not easy, it nevertheless can be done".

3.   Henri Nouwen

In this chapter, I could have written about many individuals. My first two choices are understandable. My third choice could have been an eminent scientist, politician or theologian but I surprised myself by choosing Henri Nouwen. Why? The answer is complicated but probably relates to the uncertainty and struggles that he has had with his beliefs. It was an important contrast to the certainty of the Roman Catholic Mother Teresa or the Buddhist Dalai Lama.

The first book of Henri Nouwen that I read was: "Can you drink the cup?" (1996). This small book has been reprinted five times. While at a morning service, Nouwen heard the question: "Can you drink the cup?" (Matthew 20.22). The question was Jesus' answer to the mother of Zebedee's sons who had asked for her sons to sit at his right and left hand in the Kingdom of God. His full question was "Can you drink the cup that I am going to drink?" Nouwen's wonderfully written book states "drinking the cup of life involves holding, lifting and drinking". He concluded "when we drink the cup as Jesus drank it we are transformed into one body of the living Christ, always dying and always rising for the salvation of the world".

The second Nouwen book that I read was "The Genesee Diary – Report from a Trappist Monastery" (1989). I liked this book for its sincerity and it is about something I have wanted to do. After years of "restless searching", this book records his seven months living as a Trappist monk. At the Abbey of the Genesee, the Abbot was John Eudes: "not only a listener but also a guide, not only a counsellor but also a director". Nouwen then makes the statement: "It did not take me long to realise that this was the man I had needed". He has frequent meetings with John Eudes and learns much from this wise man.

Nouwen had entered the monastery to be "alone with the Alone". But then recognised that "the contemplative life is like hearing a different drummer". He did not find the isolation easy and found he needed to write and receive letters; his need to communicate meant that "often a thought led to a prayer and a prayer to a letter and a letter to a real feeling of peace and warmth". He recognises that "solitude indeed makes you more sensitive to the good in people".

A large part of this book focuses on the direction given by the Abbot, John Eudes. The Abbot is a blunt man. He tells Nouwen: "It is not surprising that you are easily depressed and tired. Much of your energy is invested in keeping your hostilities and aggressions under control and in working on your appearances of gentleness and kindness". Nouwen learns from these harsh words; I felt that at least I could not have similar things said of me – appearances of gentleness is not something that I do. John Eudes also made another telling observation: "If you cannot be detached from all you do and like to do, you cannot live a full spiritual life". This observation convinced me that I could not easily live in a monastery.

Conclusion

This chapter is about three remarkable people who have lived during the time that I was following my quest for God in my daily life. Mother Teresa demonstrated her faith by her actions. The Dalai Lama showed compassion for his enemies and the absence of vengeance. Henri Nouwen was a great writer who could be sincere and inspirational in his soul-searching. They all had to contend with the pressures of living today, but were able to make time for prayer and worship. All three individuals took part and benefited from communal worship, prayer and service. Yet my feelings appeared to exclude my being part of a church community. I recognised that many in the church struggle with church structure, government and discipline but stay within the church. Indeed, such struggles are well documented in the scriptures and are not new. However, I felt that I had to get my basics right before I could consider joining a church group.

CHAPTER FOURTEEN

CONCLUSIONS

On 11.01.2002 I was divorced. This book chronicles my religious beliefs and practices from my separation to my divorce. I had not intended to write this book: my quest was personal. Then I felt that my sons might find it of interest. As I started to write, I wondered if others might have considered a quest similar to mine, but did not have the time I had to pursue matters. I believe that whatever the circumstances, there can be good outcomes and I hope that this book is one.

1.   God's will

A major message in this book is about the advantages for someone to "pray continually". However, the full quotation is very important: "Be joyful always, pray continually, give thanks in all circumstances for this is God's will for you in Christ Jesus" (1 Thessalonians 5.16-18). My feelings on joy and prayer are as in Chapter Six. I have come to believe that being joyful always is a natural end-product of continuous prayer. Thus, the first two parts of this quotation are interlinked and have been the object of most of my study. I had accepted the last part of the quotation as what one might have expected from an all-powerful God. Therefore, it was a great shock when I received an official complaint from a patient about this quotation. She occasionally attended church but could not accept that God would want her to have a disease, and she was upset that I had used the quotation. In my counselling of patients with Post Viral Fatigue Syndrome, many who attended church had benefited from this quotation. However, this complaint forced me to examine this quotation in greater detail. Does God will disease? And what about an individual's free will?

I thought about these questions for a long time. Eventually, I came to the conclusion that they were inter-linked. God does allow free will and therefore things must happen that God does not want. My best explanation was that of my relationship with my sons. Many times they want to do what I do not "will". Mostly, I allow this as they have to learn and grow. I could stop these events unfolding but I choose not to. I reasoned that in the same way God "wills" all that happens to each of us. I recalled Mother Julian of Norwich (Backhouse and Pipe, 1987): "I had often wondered why, in God's foreknowledge, his wisdom could not have prevented the origin of sin. For if he had, I thought, all would have been well. Sin is necessary – but all will be well". Thus, I have found one explanation but I recognise that others may not agree.

2.   Assessment

As a scientist, I have always tried to assess my progress. Usually, it is every six months: during my summer holiday and after Christmas. Mostly, I would have achieved 3-4 objectives and 1-2 would be proving more difficult. My quest to find God in my daily life has taken seven years. And, although I have achieved some objectives, the job is not finished.

Prayer has become very much more important to me. Instead, of a few hurried minutes at the end of the day, I start my day with prayer, punctuate the whole day and finish with more prayers. I do not worry about how and what to pray. Instead, I believe that: "The holy fathers say that the Jesus prayer is the abbreviated version of the whole Bible" (Savin, 1996). However, at the start and end of the day, I also use the Lord's prayer and adopt the popular acronym ACTS. This acronym allows you to remember the important stages of prayer: Adoration, Confession, Thanksgiving and Supplication. (D'Ambrosio, 2001). Quite simply, the more I have prayed, the more I want to pray. I know that my approach would not suit everyone and many would look upon some of my prayers as too "mechanical". Yet, like as when you exercise or eat, you want to do more, so it is with me and my praying.

Over the last seven years, I have read over 60 books in my quest. In this book, I have quoted only 37. Although the Bible is counted as one book, I recognise that there are tens of thousands of books on the subject. Thus, my selection of books could have been biased. Many times, the books selected could have been influenced by what was available or how they were displayed in the stores that I visited. I could argue that this allowed my selection to be random and so scientifically valid. However, as I look over what I have read and the conclusions that I came to, I feel that there was a pattern. I firmly believe that I have approached my quest in a scientific way. If this was a scientific question, I would believe that with an assessment of all that I have done that I have arrived at an answer - the truth. This would be acceptable to me, but I would also recognise that others may want to question the process and the answers. This is what happens in science.

One friend questioned the order at which questions occurred to me. He felt that I should have started with questioning the authority of the Bible and continue, probably taking many more chapters than I have. He may have been right, but this book is a documentation of what happened to me. I also accept that my quest may not seem very logical, but sometimes progress in science can be made by apparently illogical steps.

Another important criticism of my work is that it uses authors that are generally conservative. Would it have been better if the authors were more radical and less accepting of the status quo? Indeed, one friend on reading my manuscript recommended a list of books that he felt I should read. These books were very interesting and would probably enhance my book, but they were not the ones that influenced me.

My friends frequently asked: who do you expect to read this book? Initially, I felt that the readers may be disaffected members of Christian Churches. However, as I progressed, I recognised that my quest is very unlikely to be the way that many would choose. There are many ways to the top of the mountain, and mine seemed too haphazard and time-consuming. I am forced to conclude that my journey and end-result would not appeal to many. My way to the mountain top is too hazardous and the path can only take one or two. Thus, this book probably shows a path that cannot be widely used, but it may be useful to know that it exists.

My study continues and I have a stack of books to read. The constant question is: should I join an established church? For the moment, the answer is that I am not ready to accept the discipline of a church. Yet, I know that I should have a need for community and the Biblical teaching for communal worship is strong. My reluctance can be seen as a great weakness and perhaps it is. Many would have tried to find an appropriate church at the outset; and their journey would not have taken 7 years. In my decades of scientific research, I have always felt that I had an advantage in being able to assess data in less obvious ways. I also enjoyed not being influenced by groups of people. My quest has reflected my idiosyncratic approach to science.

3.   The Future

For the future, I shall continue my present practice of using my chokti, chanting and candles. Over very difficult times, both at work and at home, these have been tried and tested. I have found greater peace than I have ever known. With this peace, I have found that I have changed. Without knowing it, I had adopted the advice that Abbot John Eudes had given Henri Nouwen (1989). In a very precise way, Henri Nouwen was told that he "should be more concerned with writing than with speaking, more with studying than with counselling, more with praying than with social life". Instinctively, over the last seven years, I have adopted this advice. I do not

104

regret it.

I know that I have not reached the end of the road. There will be more questions and I shall have to search for more answers. My faith, understanding and life will continue to evolve, as the learning process continues. I sincerely hope that my faith will remain as strong as it is now. I cannot hope for more. My scientific training has helped me in my quest to have God in my daily life. Yet, I am sure that many could have walked a similar path without scientific training. It is a matter of using the gifts that we have: "We have different gifts, according to the grace given us" (Romans 12.6).

BIBLIOGRAPHY

1.	Backhouse H, Pipe R (1987) "Revelations of Divine Love – Mother Julian of Norwich" Hodder and Stoughton: London.
2.	Beckett W (1995) "Meditations on Joy" Darling Kindersley: London.
3.	Benenate B (1997) ed "In the heart of the world: thoughts, stories and prayers" New World Library: California.
4.	Benenate B, Durepos J (1997) eds "Mother Teresa – no greater love" New World Library: California.
5.	Benn W (1996) "The Last Word" Christian Focus Publications: Fearn.
6.	Bible "The NIV study Bible: new international version" (1991) Hodder and Stoughton: Kent.
7.	Blaiklock EM (1981) "The Practice of the Presence of God" by Brother Lawrence, Hodder and Stoughton: London.
8.	Bounds EM (1979) "Power through prayer" Moody Press : Chicago.
9.	Burton-Christie D (1993) "The Word in the Desert" Oxford University Press: New York.
10.	Bruce FF (1977) "Paul: Apostle of the Free Spirit" Paternoster Press: Carlisle.
11.	Bruce FF (2000) "The New Testament Documents – Are they reliable?" Inter-Varsity Press: Leicester.
12.	Clements R (1994) "The strength of weakness" Christian Focus Publications: Fearn.

13. Dalai Lama, Cutler HC (1998) "The Art of Happiness" Hodder and Stoughton: London.
14. D'Ambrosio M (2001) "Exploring the Catholic Church" Hodder and Stoughton: London.
15. Fearon M (1994) "A Breath of Fresh Air" Eagle: Guildford.
16. Gass R, Brehony K (1999) "Chanting: discovering spirit in sound" Broadway Books: New York.
17. Gledhill R (1996) "The Times: Best sermons for 1996" Cassell: London.
18. Gledhill R (1998) "The Times: Best sermons for 1998" Cassell: London.
19. Gruen A (1999) "Heaven Begins Within You" The Crossroad Publishing Company: New York.
20. Harp D (1997) "The 3 minute meditator" Butler and Tanner: London.
21. Jeffery P, Milton O (1993) "Firm Foundations" Evangelical Press of Wales: Bridgend.
22. Johnston W (1984) "The Wounded Stag" Fount Paperbacks: London.
23. Lewis CS (1979) "Surprised by Joy" Collins, Fount Paperbacks: Glasgow.
24. Morrice W (1997) "Hidden Sayings of Jesus" SPCK: London.
25. Murdock M (1984) "One-minute Pocket Bible" Honor Books: Tulsa.
26. Nouwen HJM (1989) "The Genesee Diary – report from a Trappist Monastery" An Image Book: New York.
27. Nouwen HJM (1996) "Can you drink the cup?" Ave Maria Press: Notre Dame.
28. Proto L (1989) "The alpha plan" Penguin Books: London.

29. Ringma C (1992) "Dare to journey with Henri Nouwen" Albatross Books: Australia.
30. Saunders EP (1991) "Paul – a very short introduction" Oxford University Press: Oxford.
31. Savin O (1996) "The Way of a Pilgrim" Shambhala Publications: Boston.
32. Spencer M (2000) "Athos. Travels on the Holy Mountain" Azure: London.
33. Trott S (1998) "The Holy Man's Journey" Arkana, Penguin Books: London.
34. White R (1989) "Meet St Paul" Bible Reading Fellowship: London.
35. Williamson M (1994) "Illuminata: thoughts, prayers, rites of passage" Random House: London.
36. Wilson AN (1997) "Paul. The mind of the Apostle" Sinclair-Stevenson: London.
37. Wright T (1997) "What Saint Paul Really Said" Lion Publishing: Oxford.

BETTER RECOVERY FROM VIRAL ILLNESSES

(ISBN 0-9511090-5-7)

by Dr Darrel Ho-Yen

The first edition of this book was the first book published (April 1985) on Post Viral Fatigue Syndrome (M.E., Royal Free Disease, Chronic Fatigue Syndrome). The 2nd edition was published in 1987; the 3rd edition was published in 1993 (reprinted in 1994); and the 4th edition in 1999 (reprinted in 2003).

Over the years the author has given many lectures throughout Britain and this book contains 35 illustrations in 240 pages. **The lay-out is designed for those with a limited concentration span.**

Unlike other books, this book provides a five step plan for better recovery which has been used by very many patients. This book is a product of the collective experiences and recovery of these patients. **It provides the information and motivation for the patient to recover.**

Obtainable from: **Dodona Books**
www.dodonabooks.co.uk

Unwind!

Understand and control life, be better!

(ISBN 0-9511090-2-2)

by Dr Darrel Ho-Yen

Many individuals are having great difficulties in living in a modern society. The stress on these people may produce ill health. This book shows that stress can be reduced by the acquisition of skills. **This book was first published in 1991 and reprinted in 1994.**

The skill of unwinding (EMBME) is explained in great detail and has benefits of physical and mental relaxation. **Both well and ill individuals would benefit from this skill.**

With the ability to unwind, you can start to develop an understanding of your life and identify your own problems. Control of your life is achieved by good use of time, use of the reward/effort ratio and good decision-making. **With the acquisition of these skills, you have the opportunity for self-improvement, happiness and to be better.**

Obtainable from: **Dodona Books**
www.dodonabooks.co.uk

Climbing Out of The Pit of Life

(ISBN 0-9511090-4-9)

by Dr Darrel Ho-Yen

The pit of life may be many things: death of a loved one, the end of a relationship, severe illness, financial ruin, a severe accident, betrayal, public humiliation, loss of a job or an enforced change of life.

How do some people recover quickly whilst others may never recover? How does one cope with these crises? The ladder (**l**ifeless, **a**nger, **d**enial, **d**isgrace, **e**ndeavour, **r**enewal) describes the stages one needs to go through to cope with great loss.

Dr Ho-Yen describes in details what one suffers and offers clear, practical solutions to each problem. It empowers the individual to recover quickly.

Obtainable from: **Dodona Books**
www.dodonabooks.co.uk

"It is the glory of God
to conceal a matter;
to search out a matter
is the glory of kings".

Proverbs 25.2

ISBN 0-9511090-6-5

Publishers and distributors:

**Dodona Books
Corriemuir
Viewhill
Culloden Moor
Inverness
IV2 5EA**